Why I Hate My Employer

San Marcos, California

Why I Hate My Employer

If given the opportunity to relive my life all over, I would become a Spanish teacher.

BY

CHARLES F. PADGET

Why I Hate My Employer

Copyright © 2009 by Charles Frederick Padget

Library of Congress Control Number: 2008909679
ISBN-10: 0-615-23043-1
ISBN-13: 978-0-615-23043-6

To The Nines Publishing
1294 Rue St. Moritz
Suite 201
San Marcos, California 92078

Printed and bound in the United States of America

2 4 6 8 10 9 7 5 3 1

*Dedicated to the man who, at one time in his life,
told me that if I was going to open my mouth,
I ought to do so for something other than to perform
oral sex:*

CHARLES WILLIAM PADGET

*My mentor, my hero, the man whom I refer to as Dad and,
more importantly, the man whom I had always taken for
granted.*

Contents

	PREFACE	VIII
I.	THE OLDER I BECOME, THE SMARTER MY OLD MAN LOOKS	1
II.	THE WORLD'S MOST SUCCESSFUL PRACTICAL JOKE	11
III.	WHEN IN ROME ...	23
IV.	AIN'T NO RIGHT WAY TO DO THE WRONG THING	39
V.	AND IN THIS CORNER, WEIGHING IN AT ...	57
VI.	UNTIL DEATH DO US PART	69
VII.	ANCHORS AWEIGH	89
VIII.	WIN	95
IX.	CHANGE IS INEVITABLE	113
X.	IF YOU'RE NOT A PART OF THE SOLUTION, YOU'RE PART OF THE PROBLEM	123
XI.	NO MAN IS AN ISLAND	137

Preface

x

THE OPINIONS AND RECOMMENDATIONS HEREIN STATED ARE mine and mine alone. While I'm certain that others share similar views with regard to the subject of illegal immigration, I am ultimately responsible for each and every word contained within the following pages.

With that said, I feel a need to caution the reader that some consider me to be both a bigot and a racist. Others, however, might argue nothing could be further from the truth. Nevertheless, I shall remain silent and let the reader be the judge. Hopefully, after reading this book, the reader shall be able to determine on his own whether it was based upon race or simply upon the facts.

Those who are opposed to this book may question my right to reduce my views to writing. It is for those people that I state the following:

Those men and women who have served before me, with me, and are now currently serving this nation within the various branches of the armed forces have provided me with this right. Let us not forget those who have paid the ultimate sacrifice.

In addition, the First Amendment to the United States Constitution accords me the right based upon the fact that I was born within the confines of the United States of America. But I don't claim this right on my birth alone. Although I saw no combat action, I voluntarily gave up almost twelve years of my life, receiving not one, but two honorable discharges from the United States Marine Corps. Unfortunately, neither of the two owners of the company that I'm currently in the employ of can claim the same. Apparently, neither of them had the time or the courage to serve. In fairness, their father served in the United States Navy for a short period of time. As to whether or not his service was voluntary, I cannot say.

Should doubt remain as to why I have the right to write this book, then someone needs to translate these words into your own language. If that is in fact the case, chances are you shouldn't be here and maybe you ought to give serious consideration to relocating back to where you came from, as the system currently in place is going to change. Hopefully, these changes aren't going to be in your favor, and this book will serve as a catalyst that moves the system in that direction.

For those who believe my sole objective in authoring this book is for financial gain, I must admit that I did not know beforehand how difficult it is to become an author. In fact, I ended up spending not only a couple of years writing this book, but also many hours of research to ensure my facts are accurate. In doing so, I, like every other American wage earner, want to be paid for my time and effort.

Again, my sincerest gratitude goes out to those who are currently abroad protecting the freedoms that I and every other American enjoy on a daily basis. Moreover, while I cannot speak for those who own the company I work for, I assume they too are grateful to those defending their right to employ illegal immigrants.

Last and certainly not least, some, after reading this book, may opine that my "anger" is directed toward one nationality, and they might be right. Although I feel no need to defend myself here, if it appears to the reader that the subject of the book is based solely on those who have illegally emigrated from the country of Mexico, it's because I live in close proximity to the Mexican border rather than any perceived hatred I have for the Mexican people. Frankly, it's the person's immigration status that is more of a concern to me than his nationality.

CHAPTER I

The Older I Become, the Smarter My Old Man Looks

(I Wanna Talk About Me)

I am who I am today because of the decisions that I have either made or not made throughout the course of my life.
Charles F. Padget, American wage earner and veteran

BEFORE DELVING INTO THE HEART OF THE SUBJECT MATTER OF this book—which you will soon discover is about the history, cause, and my recommended solutions concerning the illegal immigration problem currently facing this nation—I want to give the reader some brief insight as to not only who I am but also the predicament I have gotten myself into as an American wage earner.

Specifically, I am nothing more than an average wage earner who, with the exception of the time I spent defending this country as a United States Marine, has spent his entire working career helping others get rich. Moreover, after reading this book in its entirety, it should become evident, with my poor use of grammar and numerous run-on sentences, that I possess no more than a high school education. Despite my lack of formal education, I am, however, cognizant of the fact that my situation is not unique and, in fact, thousands, if not millions, of other American wage earners have gotten themselves into the same predicament. Nevertheless, the following is my story:

As a child growing up in a middle-class household, I was often left to wonder who, if anyone, appointed my father God—the man of all-knowing. While in this household, I heard things such as "Do as I say, not as I do" and "There isn't anything you have done or are thinking of doing that I haven't done or thought of myself." Although my father has since passed away, nothing is more evident as to his intelligence than the fact that I'm still in the employ of the company he adamantly advised me to leave four years prior to his passing.

At the time he advised me to leave, as I did so many times before as a child, I thought the old man hadn't a clue, but he, as on every prior occasion, was right. Failing to follow my father's advice, I feel that not only have I wasted the last fourteen years of my life, but have lost something that can never be replaced—a relationship with my father.

Sometime during June 1998, I received a telephone call from my father, who resided in Rochester, New York. If my recollection is correct, I had been employed by my present employer for approximately five years and I believe I was being paid $10 per hour with a benefits package that included one week vacation and two sick days a year. Being unaware of my situation, my father requested that I return home for a visit. Further, he offered to pay for my round-trip airfare and said I could stay at his home during my visit. As so requested, I agreed to spend my vacation with him.

After hearing that I was returning home for only one week, he asked what I had done or was going to do with the remainder of my vacation time. I responded that one week was all I received from my employer. Then in the most disappointing voice I have ever heard anyone use, let alone my father, he informed me that I was either a liar or a fool to work for a company that provided only one week of vacation after five years of service. Moreover, he said that he had not raised a fool; therefore, I had to have been lying. Additionally, he stated that if coming to visit for only one week was all that I thought of him, then there was really no need to come at all.

He then abruptly terminated the phone call by hanging up. Sadly, those were the last words I ever heard him utter. In August 2002, I was notified of his passing.

Almost ten years have passed since my father advised me to leave this company and, much to my dismay, not much has changed. In fact, I'm currently making $14 per hour (one $2 raise over the past seven years) with a benefits package that still includes only one week vacation and two sick days per year.

Surely, there must be a logical reason as to why a man of almost forty-nine years would consider a job that pays so little a career. It's possible, I guess, that someone in a position such as mine could become comfortable with his or her surroundings and feel compelled to stay out of fear of possibly not being able to obtain employment elsewhere. It also can be said that someone such as I might believe that his or her hard work will eventually pay off in the end with a good-paying position. However, in the same breath, it also must be said that there comes a time when that same individual must realize that the pot of gold (great paying position with numerous benefits) is nothing more than a pipe dream.

So, why then would an employer pay a man with more than fourteen years of continuous service so little? I, for one, fully understand that the only way employers can make a profit is by paying individuals they employ less than they produce. Should they choose to pay an individual as much as or more than he or she can produce, their company would then either break even or operate at a loss. If that were in fact the case, the employers themselves would be looking for employment elsewhere. But that, in my opinion, is where common and good business sense leave off and fairness takes over.

Throughout my career in the United States Marine Corps, I attended several military and civilian management courses.

It is where I discovered that Marines who are "happy," so to speak, fight harder and those civilian employees who are treated well produce more. Therefore, it only stands to reason that the more their employees produce, the more profit the employers make. On the reverse side of the coin, an employee such as I cannot, in all fairness to the employer, produce the least amount expected and then turn around and expect to be paid more.

In my opinion, when deciding to either promote and/or pay an employee more, the employer should consider the employee's previous experience, time of continuous service with his company, as well as the employee's overall performance. For example, in the Marine Corps, individuals receive, depending upon his or her rank, either proficiency and conduct marks or yearly fitness reports that are then used to determine promotion as well as pay raises. Recently, I have been told that many companies within the civilian sector perform semi-annual and annual personnel evaluations in order to determine whether or not an individual is to be promoted and possibly paid more.

Furthermore, I was told that any favorable or derogatory information contained within the employee's personnel file is also taken into consideration. Additionally, I was led to believe that if anything derogatory in nature is going to be placed into an individual's personnel file, that individual is, by law, accorded the right to either agree with such information or is given an opportunity to rebut it in writing. In my case, with the exception of a talk given by one of the owners of my company at the beginning of each year about what he believes the company needs to achieve and the goals he has set for me for the coming year, I have not, to the best of my knowledge, ever been the subject of a personnel evaluation. I am also not aware of anything derogatory in nature that has been or is going to be placed into my personnel file, should one exist. I have, however, gotten my fair share of verbal "ass chewings."

So, before I can assign blame elsewhere for being paid only $14 an hour, I first must consider the actions of the man I see in the mirror each and every morning. A position of more than fourteen years of continuous service can hardly be considered an entry level position (one that requires little or no experience to perform) nor should it be paid as little as most employers in the area pay such a position. This being the case, I must opine the reason why I'm being paid so little is that for the past fourteen years my work performance has been substandard. However, if my performance has truly been substandard, why then would my employer keep me for such a long period of time? The answer is, he wouldn't. So I now can safely rule out my work performance as the reason why I'm paid so poorly.

Another reason could be that I possess a poor or tardy attendance record. Considering during the past fourteen years I have missed only one day of work without authorization, utilized one sick day and one week of authorized personal time (without pay) in order to put my father's affairs in order after his death, I can say for certain that my attendance record cannot and should not be a factor. Moreover, with regard to any tardiness, I note for the record that my residence is located within the building where I work, so if anything, I was early more often than on time.

The only other reason I can think of as to why I'm being paid so poorly is because I possess a criminal record. Before being hired, I informed my employer that I had, on one occasion, been convicted of operating a motor vehicle in the state of California while under the influence of alcohol or drugs. Additionally, I was convicted of a couple of other offenses not related to my job on a few other occasions during my employment, and, while under no obligation to do so, informed my employer, who has retained my services nevertheless. My record does not, however, thanks to several thousands of dollars and a couple of good lawyers, indicate that I have ever been convicted of a felony or a crime involving moral turpitude.

If anything, my employer certainly could use my criminal record as justification for paying me poorly. However, with the exception of missing one day due to being confined awaiting arraignment for a second driving under the influence charge that occurred almost thirteen years ago, I have not missed any work due to any misconduct on my part. Should this be his justification, my response is that what I do on my own time is of no one's concern other than my own as long as it does not, in any way, shape or form, affect the performance of my duties. If there is, in fact, a personnel file being maintained on me, it will show that my off-hours misconduct has not affected my job performance in any way.

Now that I have reasonably ruled out anything I have done as a logical reason for my being so poorly paid, I can in good faith look elsewhere to assign blame. But who or what is to blame for my predicament? Hopefully you've guessed it: My company and those who own it are to blame. Obviously, paying someone poorly is neither unlawful nor a reason to hate them; it is, however, in my opinion, a very good reason to dislike them.

But dislike is not what this book is all about. It's about my hatred for this employer. Some at this point may be thinking my rationale for this hatred is the result of losing a relationship with my father. Nothing could be further from the truth. If anyone is responsible for such a loss, it's me. I could have—and regret not doing so—taken the advice of my father and left this company years ago. More importantly, nothing prevented me, after cool heads prevailed, from picking up the phone and calling him. Instead, without any such promise from my employer, I chose to stay in hopes that someday I could write my own ticket.

So, while I have a very good reason to dislike my employer, I have but one to hate him. Simply put:

My employer employs more illegal immigrants than American citizens. Even if he had employed only one such individual, I'd still hate him.

That being said, I can say with certainty that if this book is read by my employer, he will, as many other employers have done to others, label me as a disgruntled employee, which, quite frankly, is all right by me. In fact, I would again, if given the chance, defend his right to say such.

For those who are reading this book who have gotten themselves into the same predicament as I have gotten myself into, I hope your situation changes. For those of you who currently employ illegal immigrants, I hope that you cease doing so. I hope that my employer, after labeling me a disgruntled employee, realizes that it's not all about him. I hope that someone who is currently holding a political position and may be reading this book be courageous enough to submit for approval a bill that either reflects or is very similar to either of my recommendations that I have set forth at the end of this book. And for those of you who have yet to enter the work force, I hope you listen to the advice of your parents, who may just know something.

Recently, someone who is aware of my current employment and also knows I am authoring this book asked what, if anything, would I do differently with regard to my employment if I had the chance to do it all over again. At the time of his question, I really had no answer for him. However, if he were to ask me at this moment, I would without any hesitation tell him that upon the expiration of my enlistment in the United States Marine Corps, I would have gone back to school to further my education in order to become a Spanish teacher.

CHAPTER II

The World's Most
Successful Practical Joke

(Beware of Greeks Bearing Gifts)

Should this nation choose not to alter its course with regard to illegal immigration, it shall soon reduce itself to nothing more than a punch line to a very old joke.
Charles F. Padget, American wage earner and veteran

To some, few things in life make them laugh more than a well-planned, well-executed practical joke. Throughout the years, children, college students (MIT gets honorable mention here), business associates, and, most notably, radio disc jockeys have planned and executed all sorts of practical jokes. The practical joke is not, however, limited to individuals, as countries have even been known to occasionally pull one off.

By definition, a practical joke is a situation set up usually to produce what the initiator imagines to be a humorous outcome at the expense of the chosen target (victim). This joke is distinct from a verbal or written joke in that its goal is to make physical events appear miscalculated, inept, or just plain stupid. Afterward, the deception is then revealed to the target, with the intention of making him or her feel foolish or victimized.

Despite the expression "It's only funny until someone gets hurt; then it's hilarious," it is unfathomable for me to think that anyone who possesses the ability to comprehend the purpose of a practical joke would then subsequently plan and execute such with the intention of causing grievous bodily harm. However, sometimes no matter how many precautions the initiator may take to ensure injury or death does not occur, neither he nor anyone else can predict for certain the future, yet alone the outcome of his joke.

For instance, the initiators of the world's most successful practical joke had no way of knowing at the time of execution that it would become a major contributing factor to one of this nation's greatest tragedies, what this nation now commonly refers to as 9/11. I'm not making light of those who lost their lives by implying this tragedy was nothing more than a practical joke. I do, however, believe the chances of that tragedy happening would have been greatly diminished had the world's most practical joke not been executed nearly 140 years earlier.

If it was the initiators' intention to cause harm to this nation with their joke, they, despite the effect it had on 9/11, failed miserably. While many Americans feel this event hurt this nation greatly, I must demur. In my opinion, it served as a wake-up call to a nation that had up until that horrible day taken its freedoms for granted. Those who died did not do so in vain. Instead, their deaths have caused this nation to now take certain precautions to prevent any further tragedies such as the one that occurred on 9/11.

While many practical jokes are humorous, the effects of some can be dangerous and greatly impact society. Nevertheless, although a practical joke can be defined, I am unaware of any "rating system" currently in place to measure its effectiveness. In lieu of such a system and for the purpose of this chapter, I have come up with a system of my own.

In doing so, I have taken into account the joke's absurdity, notoriety, and most importantly, the number of people taken in by it. Listed below are what I believe, with the exception of the world's most successful practical joke, to have been the most humorous and had the greatest impact upon society. They have been listed in reverse order as to what I believe to be their effectiveness.

On October 30, 1938, between the hours of 8 p.m. and 9 p.m., people in New York City and its surrounding areas left their homes. Some even took refuge in nearby parks. Thousands of others called the police, radio stations, and newspapers in New York as well as other cities in the United States and Canada. They sought advice as to how to protect themselves against the raids that were currently taking place. The question was, who or what were these people seeking protection from? They sought protection from nothing more than Orson Welles' adaptation of H.G. Wells' "The War of the Worlds," which had just been broadcast on CBS and its affiliated radio stations.

During 1985, a story was published in the April edition of Sports Illustrated about a rookie pitcher who planned to play baseball for the New York Mets. It seemed as if this kid, whose name was Sidd Finch, could throw a baseball at the speed of 168 miles per hour with pinpoint accuracy. More amazing, the article pointed out, was that he had never played the game of baseball; instead, he mastered the "art of the pitch" in a Tibetan monastery under the guidance of the great poet-saint Luna Milaraspa. Baseball fans flooded Sports Illustrated with calls for more information regarding this prodigy only to discover this kid existed only in the imagination of writer George Plimpton.

In 1957, "Panorama," the respected BBC news show, informed the people of England, during one of its broadcasts, that due to a very mild winter coupled with the virtual elimination of the dreaded spaghetti weevil, Swiss farmers were enjoying a bumper spaghetti crop. Further, this story was accompanied by footage of Swiss peasants pulling strands of spaghetti down from trees. Many called the program inquiring how they too could grow their own spaghetti trees. The BBC diplomatically replied that the callers should place a sprig of spaghetti in a tin of tomato paste and hope for the best.

As you can see, the humor and effectiveness varied in each case. The first example had a major U.S. city in panic for hours, the second had the attention of the entire baseball nation, especially those of us who are Yankee fans, and the third practically duped an entire country. I assure you, however, that these jokes pale in comparison to what I now refer to as the world's most successful practical joke. Not only is the impact of this joke still felt today, it has essentially duped the entire world.

If I had to venture a guess, most Americans are of the belief that England has had the most influence upon our nation. Should my assumption be correct, those Americans would be wrong. I believe it is the French who have had, and will continue to have, the greatest effect on this nation. Our relationship with France dates as far back as the Revolutionary War. Chances are, had the French Navy not assisted General George Washington, I wouldn't be sitting here writing this book.

More recently, France has incurred the wrath of the American people over its stand on the war in Iraq. Regardless whether or not this wrath is justified, it should have been directed toward them as far back as 1886. This was not only the year that the world's most successful practical joke was executed, but it was during this same period that I believe immigrants started entering this country unlawfully. Although it is my contention that it is the greed of the American employer that has caused the problem of illegal immigration to flourish, the French are ultimately responsible as the result of their practical joke.

In 1876, the French government commissioned Frederic Bartholdi to design a sculpture to be given as a gift to the United States to commemorate the centennial of the signing of its Declaration of Independence. It has been said that

Bartholdi modeled this sculpture after Libertas, the ancient Roman goddess of freedom from slavery, oppression, and tyranny. The deal, as I understand it, was a joint venture between the United States and France.

The United States agreed to build and finance the base for the sculpture, while the French were responsible for the sculpture and its subsequent assembly. The construction of the sculpture was completed in July 1884, and it arrived in New York Harbor, in pieces ready for assembly, aboard the French frigate Isere on June 17, 1885. Due to the fact that the construction of the pedestal would not be completed until April 1886, this "gift" had to be stored in wooden crates for eleven months.

On October 28, 1886, after declaring the day a holiday, President Grover Cleveland unveiled to the world the world's most successful practical joke. Apparently we thought so much of this sculpture that for many years subsequent to its unveiling, it was used as nothing more than a lighthouse. This all changed in 1924, the year that President Calvin Coolidge declared this sculpture a national monument, what we now refer to as the Statue of Liberty, but what I believe was a "Trojan horse."

Before stating my rationale for labeling the Statue of Liberty as nothing more than a practical joke, I want to bring to light how little the measures we utilized up until 9/11 to secure this nation have changed from those that were in place at the time of the unveiling of the Statue of Liberty.

Specifically, many, if not most, Americans are of the belief that President Bush and his administration are to blame for the events that occurred on September 11, 2001. It is also my understanding that these same individuals believe that either President Bush or a member within his administration had prior knowledge that such an attack was imminent and, despite this, failed to act upon it. Although I have serious reservations about whether this is true, if it were, President Bush's actions were no different from those taken by President Cleveland prior to his unveiling of the Statue of Liberty.

During 1884, Cleveland, then the governor of the state of New York, vetoed a bill that would have authorized the use of $50,000 of the American people's money to pay for the remaining construction costs of the pedestal for the Statue of Liberty. I was unable during my research of this subject to find Cleveland's reason for vetoing this bill. It could have been as simple as his thinking the money could be better spent elsewhere, or maybe it's possible he did so because he had information that the statue may be a risk to the security of this nation. Should the latter be the case—that President Cleveland unveiled the Statue of Liberty despite having information it might pose a threat to this nation's security—then those blaming President Bush for the events of 9/11 may now want to blame Cleveland and his administration.

Nevertheless, shortly afterward, and in order to raise funds, those responsible for the completion of the pedestal held an auction in which they auctioned off the "The New Colossus," a sonnet written in the year 1883 by poet Emma Lazarus. The reason as to why they chose this sonnet is unknown to me. Also unknown to me is whether or not those who chose this sonnet conducted what we would now consider to be a background check on Ms. Lazarus.

Although she was born an American, it is my understanding after reading many of her works that her loyalty lay elsewhere. In my opinion, she was more concerned with the plight of those living outside of the United States. Failure to conduct such a background check at that time not only severely compromised the security of this nation, but contributed to as well as encouraged illegal immigration.

When determining whether or not the Statue of Liberty is nothing more than a practical joke, one only needs to focus upon Bartholdi's choice of metal in making his sculpture, as well as the words contained within Lazarus' sonnet. Specifically, Bartholdi's decision to use copper may have been based upon ease of use, effectiveness of cost, lack of corrosion, and/or its availability.

I am, however, of the belief that both Bartholdi and the French government had another idea in mind. It's my belief that they believed that we would be so in awe of its size and beautiful color that we would overlook the properties of the metal of which it was made. Apparently, that is exactly what we did. Those familiar with the properties of copper are well aware that its original beautiful reddish-orange color will, after time and being subjected to adverse weather conditions, change.

With regard to Ms. Lazarus' sonnet, I now know, and hopefully you do as well, that what we were taught as children that "sticks and stones may break our bones, but words (names) will never hurt us" was nothing more than a lie. People have lost relationships and countries have gone to war over nothing but words.

The following are the infamous words as written by Ms. Lazarus that were inscribed on a bronze plate that currently hangs upon a wall within the pedestal of the Statue of Liberty:

Give me your tired, your poor,
Your huddled masses yearning to breathe free,
The wretched refuse of your teeming shore.
Send these, the homeless, tempest-tost to me ...

···········

I believe it is these words that caused innocent Americans to be killed and are now being used as an invitation to those who are currently entertaining the idea of coming to this country illegally in hopes of a better life.

The reader at this point may be asking himself what could either of the two points immediately stated above have to do with the Statue of Liberty as being a practical joke. At the beginning of this chapter, I set forth what I believed to be the true definition of a practical joke, which would be deception. But how did both Bartholdi and the French government deceive us?

They deceived us by using copper, knowing that over time, it would eventually turn green, which we now know is the color of the almighty American dollar. Moreover, it's possible that Ms. Lazarus' words were chosen at the suggestion of the French government in order to assist in the execution of their practical joke.

If a practical joke was not what they had in mind, they very well could have chosen to give us the statue already heavily weathered (green in color) with a very large neon sign that read:

*Come on over, you're the next contestant
on "Who Wants to Be a Millionaire?"*

Which is exactly the point I feel they were attempting to convey. But in the same breath, they knew had they done just that, we not only would have not accepted it, but would not have put it up for exhibition in order for the whole world to see. However, I am not the first to figure this out. The French may have duped us at first, but at some point between the years of 1924 and 1962, the United States government came to this same realization.

Had they not come to this realization, then in 1962, I believe that the United States government would have purchased a monument from the country of England and had it transported here. They would then have reconstructed it so that it would reach from Ellis Island to Europe. That way, those wishing to come here illegally could do so with greater ease. Instead, this monument was privately purchased by an American investor who had it transported to Lake Havasu, Arizona, where London Bridge remains today.

Hopefully, the reader has taken this chapter in the manner in which it was intended. Although I believe that what I have stated above could very well be true, it is my sole intention to shed some light humor upon a very serious and sad problem currently facing this nation.

In addition, I noticed that while typing this manuscript from my handwritten notes, I had, for whatever reason, abbreviated the Statue of Liberty as SOL, an acronym that is used by many when referring to someone as being "shit out of luck." SOL is indeed what this nation shall become should it not in the not too distant future solve the problem of illegal immigration it now faces.

CHAPTER III

When in Rome...

(Friendly Advice to Those Here Attending Our Party
With or Without an Invitation)

Every immigrant who comes here should be required within five years to learn English or leave the country.
Theodore Roosevelt, U.S. president

WHEN IN ROME, DO AS THE ROMANS DO. IF BY CHANCE YOU don't or are unable to understand this statement, then hopefully I shall within the coming pages be able to put it into terms that you'll clearly understand. Simply put, when visiting a foreign country, ours in particular, whether it be for vacation and/or at the invitation of that country for employment, be respectful of that country's customs, traditions, and laws.

Prior to my enlistment in the Marine Corps, the only other country I had the pleasure of visiting was Canada. At the time of those visits, I was not only too young to do anything other than what I was told to do by my parents, but was far too young to fully comprehend and/or appreciate the opening statement. That did, however, all change upon my graduation from Marine Corps Boot Camp located at Parris Island, South Carolina, in the fall of 1978.

Shortly after graduation, I was shipped off to Marine Corps Base, Camp Pendleton, California, where I was to be trained as a legal services specialist. Camp Pendleton, for those of you who might not be aware, is located within San Diego County approximately 35 miles to the north of the United States and Mexico border. At the time of my arrival, the "in spot"—or shall I say "party town"—for young Marines, sailors, and those students attending the local learning institutions was Tijuana, Mexico, a ten-minute walk (should one choose to do so) beyond the Mexican border. Before my first liberty (authorized time off), my unit was assembled in formation and was subsequently addressed by our commander, whose name currently escapes me, regarding the possible dangers associated with traveling abroad. He also reminded us that when doing so, we were not only a guest of that country, but as a United States Marine, we were, in effect, a representative of the United States of America. Further, he stated it was imperative that each and every one of us be on our best behavior by being respectful of that country's customs and traditions and by obeying its laws.

In January 1986, I was again the subject of yet another permanent change of station (commonly referred to as PCS within the miliary community). This time, I was being transferred to the lst Marine Aircraft Wing, which was at that time, and I am led to believe that it is still, located in Iwakuni, Japan.

Upon my arrival, I and those who were with me on that extremely long eighteen-hour plane flight were temporarily assigned to the indoctrination center while we awaited orders to our respective units. During our time there, we were schooled on Japanese law and were given an extensive course on the country's history, customs, and traditions. Moreover, it had been highly suggested, I assume to make our tour of duty much more enjoyable, that we make every effort to learn as much of their language as possible—a suggestion I would later come to regret not taking.

Approximately halfway through my tour of duty, I decided to spend the annual leave that I had accrued the year before with my fiancee, Patti (now my ex-wife), who also was a Marine, stationed in Washington, D.C., while attending the Marine Corps Legal Services Reporters Course. In that I had only thirty days of leave (vacation days), I wanted to spend as much time with her that I could. Therefore, I waited until the last possible moment before returning to my unit in Japan. In doing so, I cut my return so close that had I missed just one connecting flight, even if the next flight to the same destination were to have left only ten minutes later than the one I had missed, I would have been unable to arrive back at my unit at the time prescribed. I then would have been considered to be in a UA (unauthorized leave), also known as AWOL (absent without leave), status.

My initial flight went well, so well that I was able to make both connecting flights without a hitch. The only thing I had left to do to ensure that I returned back to my unit on time was to take the next Shin train, which at that time was known as the world's fastest train. Unfortunately, I had failed to take into account the fact that I hadn't a clue as to the location of the train station in relation to the airport.

Consequently, any success I would have had in catching the train on time rested solely on finding someone who both spoke and comprehended English. I was left with asking both those who passed by as well as the many local merchants. To my detriment, I soon discovered that everyone I had stopped and asked spoke little or no English. Those who did, spoke very little and seemed limited to "hi," "bye," and "thank you."

Finally, in my search for the train station, I happened to come upon a Japanese policeman, who I was certain spoke English and would undoubtedly provide me with directions to the train station. I was SO wrong. For approximately twenty minutes, I attempted to ascertain the location of the train station by not only speaking English but utilizing every arm motion imaginable. Every attempt, however, became a failure.

Totally frustrated, I then turned around and started to walk away. As I was walking away, I heard the policeman say in clear and unbroken English, "Have a nice day, sir. I hope you find the location of the train station in time." Unfortunately, by the time I located the train station, the last train that would have gotten me back to my unit on time had already departed. Although no disciplinary action was taken against me, I was professionally embarrassed.

Here it is, almost twenty-two years later, and I am reminded on a daily basis of my tour of duty in Japan. It seems as if the language barrier I experienced there exists here in Southern California. It also appears and has been my experience that the majority of fast-food restaurants, as well as many other companies in this area, are "manned" by individuals, who, in my opinion, possess less of a command of the English language than that of a three-year-old American child. Based upon this fact, I have, at times, spent more of my lunch hour attempting to order my meal than consuming it. It matters not that these same individuals may be legally entitled to work here; whether they are or not, they should at least be required to speak and comprehend English.

What is more alarming to me than these individuals' unwillingness to speak our language is that many of these same individuals, if not most, proudly display the flags of the countries they left to come here illegally. For example, a few years back, a protest march was held here in San Diego. This march, presumably organized by those in favor of illegal immigration, was to show their displeasure at Congress' failure to act upon a bill currently before it that, if passed, would have granted those here illegally not only immunity from prosecution but the opportunity to apply for American citizenship as well. The little that I saw of this march, I can attest that many in attendance carried the flags of the country of their origin. Although I can't say for certain, it seems to me that carrying an American flag would have been more beneficial to their cause than carrying the flag of another country.

Yet another example of where these individuals' loyalty lies is within the wide world of sports. During the World Cup in 2002, which many of us Americans now know to be the world's largest soccer tournament, I was assigned by my employer to work the graveyard shift. With the exception of me and one other, all of those assigned to work this shift were born in the country of Mexico. Out of the two of us that were not, I was the only one born within the United States. Moreover, to the best of my knowledge, I also was the only employee working here legally. Nevertheless, unbeknownst to me, the United States soccer team had been playing surprisingly well during the World Cup. So well, that if it won its next two games, it would earn the right to play in the championship game.

Shortly after reporting to my shift one evening, I was approached by one of my co-workers to ascertain whether or not I had a desire to place a bet upon that evening's game. I guess my response of "what game?" was an indication of how little I knew or, better yet, cared about the World Cup. After hearing my response, the individual who had approached me for the bet informed me that Mexico was playing the United States and that he was willing to bet me $20 that Mexico would defeat the United States. Based upon the fact that I knew nothing about either team playing and the fact that he was laughing profusely after I had accepted the bet, I figured that I pretty much "pissed" away that $20.

Apparently, word had spread on what an easy mark I was, as all of my remaining co-workers approached me wanting to make the same bet, which of course I took. To this day, I'm unsure as to why I took those bets because, as a rule of thumb, I would first have to have knowledge of the event, person, or thing I was betting on before placing any bet. If I had no knowledge whatsoever, I would do a little research before deciding whether or not I still wanted to place the bet. These bets were clearly an exception to that rule and were most likely placed with nothing more than my American pride.

As I now had $160 of my hard-earned money invested in this game, when it came time for it to start, I turned it on and played it over the shop intercom. I did so in order that everyone could hear. Much to my surprise—and, based upon their expressions, much to the surprise of those whom I had bets with—when it was all said and done, the United States had again been victorious by defeating Mexico 2 to 0, thereby earning them the right to play Germany in the next round for the chance of advancing to the championship game. Unfortunately for the United States soccer team, the magic had run its course, as they were defeated by Germany, thereby ending their tournament.

Regardless of whether or not the United States had won or lost, I couldn't help but wonder, after witnessing the expressions upon the faces of those whom I had bet, that if by chance the United States were ever to be at war with Mexico, whether these same individuals would help defend our nation or would they fight for Mexico upon our soil.

Despite the actions of those individuals, I shouldn't let, as the old saying goes, "one bad apple spoil the whole bushel." I'm pretty sure, actually I'm certain, that there are individuals who are not United States citizens who are here either legally or illegally who do, in fact, "do as the Romans do."

The one "Roman" that I do know of is a woman I have known for almost seven years. Her name is Gisela Aguilar, whom I affectionately refer to as my little "Nazi" friend. I do so because she was born and raised in the country of Germany. She came to the United States as the result of marrying an American soldier, my best friend, Bryan, who at that time was stationed there. At the end of his tour of duty, Bryan, along with his new bride, was transferred back to the United States. Gisela, as she tells it, was uncomfortable with the American way of life and therefore wanted to return to Germany. Bryan, as any other loving husband would have done in that position, not only applied for but was granted yet another tour of duty in Germany.

Upon completion of that tour of duty, Bryan was honorably discharged from the United States Army. Not wanting to return home to the United States (most likely because of the insistence of my little Nazi friend), he sought employment there. In doing so, Bryan, as Gisela had done while in the United States, did as the "Romans do," and respected Germany's customs and traditions and obeyed their laws. He also, I assume out of necessity, learned to speak their language. At some point afterward, due to an illness to Bryan's mother, they returned to the United States, where, with the exception of a few short vacations back to Germany, they have remained ever since.

Up until this point, you may think that you too know of someone such as my friend Gisela, and it's also possible some of you may think she, as so many others have done before her, married an American service member for the sole intention of obtaining United States citizenship. If you are of either opinion, I can say, without any hesitation whatsoever, that you are wrong.

Here is a woman who has not only learned our language, respects our history, customs, and traditions, but at times, has me questioning my own patriotism. Every Fourth of July, she dresses herself, children, and home in red, white, and blue, and without being asked to do so, attends with Bryan and me "West Coast Thunder," an event that is held every year at the Riverside National Cemetery. This event is held by both Harley riders and veterans in order to pay homage to those who have lost their lives defending our freedoms.

During last year's event, I discovered that Gisela knows all the words to both "The Star-Spangled Banner" and "America the Beautiful," while many of those celebrities chosen to sing the national anthem at sporting events cannot say the same, which is a crying shame. I'd like to mention one other thing about my friend Gisela. Both she and Bryan did something that neither I nor many other Americans, either because we didn't have the time or didn't care, can say they did. Upon her insistence, they both took time out of their busy schedules to attend the funeral of one of the greatest presidents this nation has ever had, Ronald Reagan.

Certainly, maybe with the exception of attending President Reagan's funeral, her actions are no more or no less than those actions we as a nation should require of both our legal and illegal "guests."

But it's not her actions that make her special and set her well apart from the rest of the pack. Although she has lived here long enough to apply for United States citizenship, she has not either applied for or received anything other than a resident alien card (green card). It is unthinkable that in this day and age that anyone who could do so would not apply for the "Holy Grail," as thousands, if not millions, of others would do just about anything to get into the United States of America in order to become a citizen.

The reason she has not done so could be as simple as she doesn't want to be a citizen or maybe she feels as if she doesn't (although I disagree) deserve to be one. I did, however, once jokingly suggest to her that if she and Bryan had ever gotten themselves into a financial hardship, she could, in order to alleviate the problem, put her "unused" citizenship up for bid on eBay.

With the exception of her understandable view on her sons not defending this country during time of war, a view I adamantly oppose, I can say without hesitation that she is by far one of the most patriotic people I have ever met. In fact, it is a pleasure to call her not only my friend, but a fellow American as well. That being said, if by chance you too have the pleasure of meeting her, I need to advise you to never, and I mean never, mention the name of Arnold Schwarzenegger within earshot of her. It will become ever so apparent, even to those who are not fluent in German, that she is not the president of the governor of California's fan club.

Back to those individuals who feel they have a right to tell us how great their country is—the country they left to come here illegally—and to fly the flag of that country: I believe they do so because of our failure as a nation to lead by example. For instance, every year on the 17th day of March, many, if not most, Americans relinquish their American citizenship in favor of becoming a citizen of the country of Ireland. On this day, these same individuals dress themselves predominantly in green, and then begin to run around yelling things such as "Kiss me, I'm Irish" and "I have the luck of the Irish."

I, along with many other Americans, know very little as to the true meaning of St. Patrick's Day. I know even less as to how it came to be here within the United States. I'm led to believe it is a national holiday within the country of Ireland. Apparently, the Irish set this day aside to celebrate the life and times of one of their patron saints, Patrick. If I had to venture a guess as to how this holiday started here, I would say it could very well have started at the suggestion of an alcoholic who felt that he or she needed yet another day to justify drinking.

I'm often left to wonder that if, for one brief moment, these "self-appointed Irishmen" ever stop to realize that by acting the way they do on that day, they are in a sense degrading a national holiday of another country. More importantly, I also wonder if these same individuals are aware of their adopted country's violent past, because if they are, they would then know that their "luck of the Irish" is dependent upon not only their religious preference but what side of the street they are standing on when the bomb explodes.

Another area in which we may have projected to those here illegally that it's OK to do what they do is in the education of our children. I cannot think of one American that I have met who was not asked, at some point during his or her education, to create a family tree.

In many cases, the roots of these so-called family trees extend beyond the borders of the United States. For some whose roots do, they for whatever reason begin displaying things such as flags to signify they are proud of their heritage. Herein lies the problem.

Those here illegally see this and then assume it's an accepted practice. Therefore, they too feel that they have the right to do so. However, what they fail to realize is that those Americans who choose to do such are not only entitled to do it in accordance with their First Ammendment right, but it's also possible that someone within their family tree may have lost his or her life defending their right to do so. If I had my way, in order to preserve our American heritage, I would require that those trees be pruned so that their roots do not extend past our borders.

But it isn't only our failure to lead by example that has sent the wrong message. It's our government's overzealous attempt to correct what some Americans today perceive as a wrong that has, in effect, sent the same message to these individuals. In an attempt to correct the perceived wrong of slavery, our lawmakers, who have been elected by popular vote, have not only dedicated an entire calendar month as Black History Month, but have even gone so far as to name a national holiday after an individual because of the color of his skin, an individual who, in my opinion, was more concerned with the plight of the few rather than the whole.

If we don't soon get a handle on the issue of illegal immigration, it won't be long, based upon the way some employers treat those whom they employ illegally, before illegal immigrants too will be demanding their own month and that our lawmakers also name a holiday after one of their leaders.

For those reading this book who are of the opinion that something like this isn't possible, I can only say that the scales of so-called justice here in San Diego are tipping that way. Specifically, I know of two grade schools in this area that have been named after that great American hero Cesar Chavez, yet again, another American who was more concerned with the plight of the few rather than the whole.

In my opinion, the message that we should have been sending all along to those here "visiting" our fine nation is as simple as the answer I received from my father as a child when I had asked him, "Why can you do it and I can't?" His response was always the same. He quickly and without any hesitation responded by saying "do as I say, not as I do!" So despite our actions, these are the words that those, whether here legally or illegally, should keep in mind before unfurling the flag of another country.

All this aside, and setting aside the fact that, in my opinion, the United States is by far the greatest nation upon this floating rock, we are far from perfect. Therefore, we can learn from our mistakes and take a page out of other countries' playbooks with regard to treating "visitors." For example, the United States could learn something from my tour of duty in Japan. As previously discussed, the Japanese made no concessions in order to make my stay there easier. In other words, I had to play by their rules or I was more than welcome to leave.

Unfortunately, we don't do that here. In fact, we cater to those who do not speak our language. So much so that a few years back someone out here in San Diego either attempted to or was successful in getting a measure on the ballot that, had this measure passed, would have made Spanish our primary language, thus making English our secondary language. I assume whoever suggested that did so because, much to my dismay, in the County of San Diego there are more people who speak only Spanish than those of us who speak only English. Instead of accommodating these individuals, we should make them speak English by not offering them any additional help whatsoever.

We can also learn from those actions as performed by my friend Gisela. If her actions have done anything, they have shown us that it is possible for someone in her situation to live within our borders as a non-citizen, and "do as the Romans do." In other words, if one person is able to do so, then it only stands to reason that the rest can and should be required to do so as well.

Before wrapping up this chapter, I want those of you who are reading this book and are here illegally to keep one thing in mind. If by chance you are one of those who feel you have the right to fly any flag you so choose and to spew statements such as "My country is better than this," "If it wasn't for us, the work wouldn't get done," and let us not forget my favorite quote, "The only real American is the American Indian," you should know that in doing so, your actions are no different from those of someone who commits murder and then turns around and brags about it. If you tell enough people just how much better your country is, then, as with that murderer, you too will eventually get caught.

In closing, for those here legally and act such as my friend Gisela acts, I say welcome. To those of you who are here illegally and who also act as Gisela does, I suggest that you return home to your country and attempt entrance legally. And for those here illegally who feel their country is so much better than ours, then I would highly suggest that you just return to your country as soon as possible.

On a more personal note, to those who are here illegally from the country immediately to our south who have accused me, as well as other Americans, of taking from you by force what we now refer to as the state of California, may I suggest that you not only pick up a history book, but that you also return home. While there, you may want to consider forming a militia and then come back with the intention of forcefully taking California back. Now, should you choose to take this course of action and attempt to take back any part of this nation that you feel is rightfully yours, then by all means do so. In fact, you not only have my best wishes but my condolences as well.

In fairness, I need to caution you that should you in fact choose this course of action, it may not work out favorably for you. Some who know me say I fear little. Those who do are in error, as the place this man least wants to be is on the wrong end of a rifle being held by an American soldier, who is not only risking his life but is also forced to spend time away from his or her family, and in some cases forced to eat food he wouldn't feed to his pets. A scorned woman has nothing on the soldier who has been placed in the above circumstances. So before making any decision, you may want to consult someone who has indeed faced that end of the rifle and ask them how well they fared.

Now, after carefully considering all of the above, you still wish to proceed with your plan to take back by force what you feel is rightfully yours, I have yet another suggestion for you. Personally, if I were stupid enough to be in your situation, I would give serious consideration to changing my religious preference to one that supposedly offers a certain amount of virgins upon death. That way, in the event your attempt is unsuccessful, you will have something to look forward to.

If you would like my advice to a more viable solution, I suggest that you return home as soon as possible and attempt to instill those freedoms you so much enjoyed while illegally in our country. Funny thing, though, you may oddly enough find out that you may not have the opportunity and/or right to do so upon your return to your own country.

Again, you indeed have my best wishes and may you too have the "luck of the Irish."

CHAPTER IV

Ain't No Right Way
to Do the Wrong Thing

(Two Sides to Every Story)

No man can rise to his greatest possible height in talent or soul development unless he has plenty of money; for to unfold the soul and to develop talent he must have many things to use, and he cannot have these things unless he has money to buy them with.
Wallace D. Wattles, American author

I pity the man who wants a coat so cheap that the man or woman who produces the cloth will starve in the process.
Benjamin Harrison, U.S. president

NOT ONLY HAVE I HEARD, BUT IT HAS ALSO BEEN MY EXPERI-ence that when there is more than one party involved, whether it be a domestic dispute, traffic accident, and so on, there is almost always two sides to every story. Occasionally, the stories coincide, but for the most part, I find that they conflict. The topic of the employment of illegal immigrants is of no exception.

History has shown us that when it comes to starting a business, many individuals go deep into debt, and in many cases, as is the case with my employer, mortgage almost everything they own. Retaining what they own is therefore heavily dependent upon the success of their business. The quicker they make a profit, the quicker they can reclaim their voluntary losses. It is this principle, I believe, that has allowed the problem of illegal immigration to flourish.

In order to expedite the recouping of their mortgaged property, these individuals seek out the illegal immigrant who is willing to work for a wage far less than the average American wage earner and, in most cases, for little or no benefits. In a nutshell, the less wages paid out, the more profit the employer makes, thus the faster he or she pays off his or her original debt. While this might appear to some to be good business sense, hiring illegal immigrants for low wages is unlawful.

Those who prescribe this business theory are no better than the woman who stands on the street corner selling her body in order to feed her children. The hiring of illegal immigrants, however, has become common practice and is thus grossly overlooked by society, unlike the aforementioned woman. Normally, society isn't concerned as to why someone breaks the law, its only concern is that he or she did. In those cases and in hopes of correcting the wrongdoing, punishment is then handed down.

In order to demonstrate exactly how much society has overlooked this problem and how lightly employers such as mine have taken the law with regard to the hiring of illegal immigrants, I need only reduce to writing a brief synopsis of the numerous conversations I have had with one of the owners of my company. We not only talked about the illegal immigration problem as a whole, but the hiring of these same individuals by our company.

During these conversations, he uttered things such as "why hire whitey, he wants too much" and "everybody else does it!" After hearing the latter statement, I then tried to ascertain as to whether or not he felt as if we would get caught, and if so, would we then be tried and, if convicted, subsequently punished. He responded by saying that until society starts enforcing the laws that are currently on the books, the chance of our being caught would be slight at best.

One morning, while reading the local newspaper, I had discovered that one of America's largest fence companies, located here in California, had been caught employing illegal immigrants. As a result, they were tried, convicted and subsequently punished. Immediately after reporting for work that day, I sought out the owner whom I had previous discussions with about the hiring of illegal immigrants to ascertain if he had heard about the fence company, to which he responded that he had.

Since he had been aware of the situation, I then asked if he now felt as if we stood a greater chance of getting caught and suffering the same fate. Not only did he tell me no, but he even went so far as to compare our hiring of illegal immigrants to a minor traffic infraction. He continued by saying that our hiring of illegal immigrants in comparison to the fence company's hiring of illegal immigrants was no different than two vehicles speeding down the freeway. Apparently, he felt as if law enforcement would go after the vehicle proceeding the fastest.

Still being unsure where he was going with this point, I asked for further clarification. He continued by saying the fence company was caught due to its very large size, and that, based upon our size (small to mid-sized company), there were many much larger companies that would get caught before we would be. He did, however, say that when these much larger companies begin getting caught, thereby bringing our misconduct to the forefront, we would then comply with the law by no longer employing illegal immigrants. Personally, I think this man needs to be commended for his willingness to obey the law if and when he is forced to do so.

Additionally, this man not only blatantly breaks the law by hiring illegal immigrants, he is also a hypocrite. Approximately ten years ago, an illegal immigrant who had been personally hired by this owner was caught removing supplies from our company that were used to make the product we produce. This individual then sold the supplies at a largely reduced rate to our competitors. When confronted about his alleged misconduct, the illegal immigrant disappeared, never to be seen again. Presumably, he returned to his native country of Mexico.

Now, as funny as this may sound, the owner responsible for hiring this individual just so happened to be the same person who reported the misconduct to the local authorities. Although I cannot say for certain, if I had to make an educated guess, I would say he had prior knowledge that the individual in question was here illegally. In my opinion, his actions indicate that he feels that it is OK for him to break the law by hiring illegal immigrants, yet it's not OK for someone to break the law by stealing from him. I'm now left to wonder, if prior to hiring this illegal immigrant, the owner was cognizant of the fact that, in a sense, he was stealing a job from a deserving American.

Unfortunately, current employment laws also promote this hypocrisy. They allow those same individuals who break the law by hiring illegal immigrants, the right if they so choose, to deny employment to an American who at some point in his or her life has been convicted of a felony. Personally, I consider that the pot calling the kettle black. It also validates the statement that "there is no honor amongst thieves."

If the truth be told, it really isn't the greed or arrogance of those who employ illegal immigrants that enrages me the most. It's the spin they put upon their misconduct. They have done such a great job of it that many Americans today are of the belief that their misconduct is good for our economy.

The sad truth of the matter is that the actions of those who choose to employ illegal immigrants are identical to those who peddle illegal drugs in order to make their living. In some, if not many, cases, the neighborhood drug dealer is better for our economy. Specifically, it has been my experience that those who make a profit from such illegal drug transactions normally spend their ill-gotten gains within their community. Doing so boosts that community's economy.

On the other hand, the same cannot be said about those who employ illegal immigrants. Shortly after receiving their compensation (paycheck) for their services from those who employ them, illegal immigrants then turn around and send a portion of their earnings abroad, presumably to family members who have been left behind. Those funds are then spent there, which we all know boosts that country's economy and not ours.

When called upon the carpet and questioned about their misconduct as well as paying those who are entitled to work here legally so poorly, those who employ illegal immigrants are the first ones to point out that no one working beneath them is being held against his or her will. While I agree that no one can "legally" be held against his will, this statement is not entirely true.

In fact, those employers are able to underpay and mistreat those they illegally employ without any fear of any real consequences. Furthermore, when it comes to employment, illegal immigrants' movements are limited to those employers who are willing to break the law by hiring them. Therefore, it is my assertion that the hiring of illegal immigrants is as close to slavery as we have come since it was abolished by President Lincoln in the mid-1800s.

In support of my assertion that those who are employed illegally are treated like slaves, I shall again use my employer as an example. Not only does this company pay them poorly, but there are a few individuals within management who have found a way to pad their own pockets at the expense of those they hire.

Because they are paid so poorly, many illegal immigrants are unable to make ends meet, and are therefore left to obtain additional funds elsewhere. Realizing how difficult or impossible it is to obtain additional employment or a loan from a lending institution without proper identification, these individuals seek out the assistance of individuals willing to lend them the funds necessary to make ends meet. Also realizing this predicament as well as the opportunity for personal financial gain, these managers agree to loan the illegal immigrant the funds requested at an interest rate and penalties that would make any loan shark envious.

On one occasion, I had the opportunity to mention to one of these "lending institutions" that I felt as if he was unnecessarily taking advantage of these people. He informed me that those who seek out his financial assistance do so on their own initiative, and should those individuals not agree with the terms of the agreement, they were more than welcome to seek assistance elsewhere—a statement, in my opinion, pretty easily made considering the illegal immigrant's predicament.

Nevertheless, just as the illusionist is able to make an elephant seem to disappear by the use of misdirection, those who employ illegal immigrants by using this same technique have been able to shift the blame of their misconduct elsewhere. Specifically, they will have you believe that it is the American consumer and the most basic of economic principles that are to blame. In their opinion, we Americans as consumers are willing to pay the least amount for the best quality item available.

At first glance, basic economics would seem to support their argument. As we all know, costs such as raw materials, utilities and machinery used, as well as payroll, are taken into consideration when setting a selling price for the item being produced. It only stands to reason that the more one pays out to produce an item, the more he has to charge in order to make a profit. Further, these employers argue, in many cases, the only cost they can control is payroll.

I cannot argue that some of what has been stated above is not true. In fact, the cost of raw materials, steel in particular, has risen dramatically because we have depleted our resources and are now purchasing them from abroad. However, no matter how correct their argument may be, it is like many other things in life—deceiving.

For example, many, if not all, mathematical problems have but one correct answer. Another answer can, however, be arrived at utilizing a different method. The following mathematical word problem is an illustration of this:

Three poker players go to Las Vegas for the night in order to play in a scheduled poker tournament. As a cost-saving measure, all three players agree to share the expense of one room. Upon check-in, they are informed that the cost of the room for one evening is $30. Each player pays the desk clerk $10 and then heads toward the room.

At some point after they check in, the hotel manager, for whatever reason, decides to give the three poker players a $5 discount off the entire cost of the room. He then summons the bellboy over to the desk. At that time, the manager then gives the bellboy five $1 bills with instructions to take them to the three poker players' room.

On the way to the room, the bellboy realizes that there were only three poker players and he has five $1 bills. Arriving at this conclusion, the bellboy decides to "pocket" two of the dollars. Upon his arrival, he then gives each of the poker players one of the remaining dollar bills.

The correct way of looking at this word problem is that when it was all said and done, the three poker players paid a total of $25 for their one night of lodging; they each received $1 back for a total of $3; and the bellboy kept $2 for himself. In other words, $25 (cost of lodging) + $3 (money refunded) + $2 (money kept by the bellboy) = $30 (money paid out originally).

It is not only the correct way to solve the above word problem, it also happens to be the way those who employ illegal immigrants want you to view their misconduct. Specifically, they will have you believe that the cost of lodging represents the money they pay out in wages and benefits; that the $3 that was refunded represents cost of material; the $2 kept by the bellboy represents the small amount of their profit; and the $30 total is the cost of their product that the American consumer in many cases is unwilling to pay.

As I have discussed earlier in this chapter, those who employ illegal immigrants want you to believe that the only cost they can control in the production of their product is the wages and benefits they pay out. This being the case and in conjunction with the American consumer's unwillingness to buy their product based upon its high cost, they are forced to either hire illegal immigrants or pay Americans poorly. With regard to their profit, they also will have you believe that they need to make such not only to stay in business, but that profit creates and maintains jobs. In a nutshell, they have us believing that their misconduct is no different and just as correct as saying $25 + $3 + $2 = $30.

Hopefully, you as the reader can now see this is nothing more than a smoke screen that those who employ illegal immigrants put up in their attempt to misdirect the blame for their misconduct upon us not only as consumers, but now as wage earners.

Despite their attempt, I am here to tell you that while we as consumers and wage earners should not be held blameless, their misconduct is not all "our" fault. If the truth be told, it is the way that all companies who employ illegal immigrants, and possibly others who do not, conduct their respective businesses and should shoulder the majority of the blame.

In order to prove my point, I shall again use the word problem as set forth above. Only this time, I will attempt to solve it the way those who employ illegal immigrants, in all reality, conduct their businesses.

Specifically, each poker player originally paid $10 for his night of lodging. Since they each received $1 back as a refund, they actually paid $9 instead of $10. So if you multiply the $9 by the number of poker players (3), the sum equals $27. Then by adding this total with the $2 kept by the bell boy ($27 + $2 = $29), you can now see that the amount of money paid out originally has been reduced from $30 to $29. So where did the other $1 go? The answer is simple. The missing $1 went into the pockets of those who employ illegal immigrants while we, as consumers and wage earners, were taking the blame for the high costs of the items being produced.

My employer is a prime example of this, as his pockets have been lined with plenty of these missing dollars. Specifically, one of the products we produce on a daily basis—after factoring in everything it costs to produce it, including wages, benefits, and cost of raw material—costs us $2 to produce (you do the math on how well this employer pays). After we produce this product, we then turn around and sell it to our vendors for anywhere from $12 to $22 per item. If my math is correct, and I believe it is, even at the lowest price of $12, my employer stands to make "only" 600 percent profit.

When any of our vendors complain about the cost of the item, my employer directs that vendor's attention toward not only the cost of material to produce the item, but the amount of money paid out in wages and benefits. Although the vendor is well aware that we are indeed making a profit on the sale, my employer is not as forthcoming with regard to exactly how much profit is being made.

Had my employer been forthcoming, it would have opened the door for the vendor to negotiate the price, thereby cutting into my employer's profit margin. Moreover, when my employer looks for yearly cost-cutting measures, instead of reducing the amount of profit he makes, he first looks at salaries and benefits being paid out.

Prior to being employed by this employer, I was of the belief that the longer you are employed, the more salary and benefits you receive. Sadly, I was mistaken. Instead of receiving more, the benefits I receive from this employer are reduced on a yearly basis. In fact, upon my employment, each employee received his or her birthday off with pay. However, as a cost-cutting measure, that privilege was eventually taken away.

Not all of the companies who employ illegal immigrants misdirect the blame for their misconduct. Some are even so bold as to tell us that employing illegal immigrants saves jobs rather than giving them away. Specifically, these employers will have us believe that they hire illegal immigrants as an alternative to relocating their entire business overseas. In their opinion, fifteen jobs are better than none.

For those of you who are reading this who are not only American wage earners but are applauding the fact that I have called to the carpet those who employ illegal immigrants, I would recommend that if by chance you are entertaining the thought of submitting an application for sainthood on my behalf, you hold off doing such, as what I'm about to say may likely change your opinion of me.

Sadly, we American wage earners have provided those who employ illegal immigrants with plenty of cannon fodder. It seems as if our so-called pride has allowed our work ethic to decline. It has declined so much that apparently we are too good to clean our own toilets, pick our own lettuce, or wash someone else's dish. Our "failure" has opened the door for those who are illegally here and willing to do so for little pay and little or no benefits.

Case in point: Our work ethic has declined so much that a movie was made mimicking it. One evening, Deborah Holland, the woman whom I had been dating at the time, suggested that I take her out for dinner and a movie. After dinner, while standing in line to purchase tickets, I overheard the couple standing at the ticket booth tell the ticket agent that they wanted to see "A Day Without a Mexican." Not knowing that it was the name of a movie currently playing and apparently without putting much thought into what I was about to say, I announced to everyone within earshot that "wouldn't we all like to see a day without a Mexican?" I can honestly say that this slip of the tongue was not made with the intent of insulting those of Mexican descent who were standing in line with me; rather, I was simply stating my opinion as to our poor work ethic.

As of this date, I have neither seen nor have had the desire to see such movie. I have, however, been told by some of those who have that the premise of the movie was to illustrate what our daily life would resort to if the Mexicans were to, for whatever reason, pack up and return home to Mexico. Apparently, we as Americans would be left to do our own dirty work. What a concept! Personally, I believe that while there may have been some illegal immigrants doing these jobs twenty years ago, I would venture to guess the majority of them were performed by us and it seems as if we got along just fine without them.

In either September or October 2007, presumably to demonstrate exactly how much we needed those who were employed illegally, someone or some organization organized what I believe was a nationwide protest. This protest, as I understand it, called for a one-day work stoppage by immigrants—illegal or not. I assume they felt that by doing so, the United States would, for a day, stop functioning.

With the exception of a few lawns not being mowed, their plan, as they soon discovered, failed miserably, although there was a possibility it might, and I use the word might loosely here, have worked had they not for weeks, and possibly months prior, broadcast their intentions over both Spanish radio and television stations. In doing so, they allowed employers such as mine, who not only spoke Spanish but regularly watched and listened to Spanish stations, to make, if necessary, plans to ensure their companies conducted business as usual.

Much to my dismay, all too often many Americans who are low-wage earners or without employment spend far too much time complaining and blaming those here who are employed illegally. The reason as to why I know this is true is that I am one of those such individuals.

Instead of taking a low-paying position or better yet furthering our education with the intent of obtaining a better-paying position, many of us are more than content to head down to our favorite watering hole to do nothing more than sit upon our asses and complain. Some say things such as "my pride won't allow me to perform that kind of job at such a low rate of pay." Yet, it is these individuals whose pride allows them to receive a handout from the system.

It is here where those who employ illegal immigrants feel as if they have hit the mother lode in justifying their misconduct. So much so that they respond to those who complain with statements such as "we tried to give you a job, but you won't take it." In other words, we as American wage earners are not only greedy, but since we are not willing to accept those poor-paying jobs, we are forcing employers to seek out those who are willing to perform them, i.e., the illegal immigrant.

Au contraire. When it comes to the employment of illegal immigrants, the American wage earners raise two very valid points. They argue that the employment of such individuals lowers wages and, in doing so, takes away jobs from deserving Americans.

First they argue that to survive, people need things and in order to get things, they first must have money. The same basic economic principle that those who employ illegal immigrants say forces them to employ such individuals can be used by the wage earner as an excuse not to perform jobs that pay poorly with little or no benefits.

In my opinion, and in comparison to the illegal immigrant, the average American wage earner needs to make more to survive. Specifically, I personally know of several illegal immigrants whose family shares a dwelling with more than one other family. In doing so, the illegal immigrant's daily living expenses are substantially lower than that of the average American wage earner, who in more cases than not, lives alone and is then solely responsible for his own expenses. Based upon this fact alone, the illegal immigrant is not only more likely but is more able to take this job than the American wage earner.

They further argue that the American wage earner cannot, in many cases, afford to take such a low-paying job. Specifically, if they choose to take such a low-paying job, which in many cases won't help the wage earner make ends meet, such a job would leave little or no time to find one that does.

Regarding their argument that the employment of illegal immigrants results in the loss of jobs, my original trend of thought was that no one or entity had the power to take away any job from any American. Then my computer suffered from a system failure. After an hour of randomly hitting keystrokes while manually removing the remainder of my hair from my forehead, I forwent my pride by calling technical support for assistance.

It is here where I first heard my new favorite catch phrase: "Hi, my name is Ackmed. You may, however, call me Fred. How may I help you, sir?" Apparently, the Dell Corporation felt as if the crashes to their systems did not cause the consumer enough aggravation. With that in mind as well as my and other Americans' "unwillingness" to pay more for their product, they were forced to relocate both their customer service and technical support divisions abroad. After conversing with Fred for approximately two hours, I now have a much better understanding of the statement, "you get what you pay for."

Unfortunately, the Dell Corporation isn't the only company that the American consumer has forced to leave the country. By calling out this next employer, I shall be stepping upon the hopes and dreams of tens of thousands of young men and women across this nation.

I too, at some point during my childhood had their dream. Despite being a Yankees fan, I had a desire to play second base for the Baltimore Orioles. In order to keep this dream intact, I spent most, if not all, of my free time practicing and playing baseball. As it turns out, all of my hard work went for naught. I decided to abandon that dream the day my mother informed me that no one ever gets rich playing baseball.

It's been twenty-one years since my mother's passing, and each year since, I have watched with an envious eye as the salaries of baseball players have skyrocketed. They have increased so much that if the likes of Babe Ruth, Hank Aaron, and Willie Mays were to be playing today, they would each have to be given their own state as their compensation for their services. As I watched, I thought to myself that my mother surely missed the boat on this one. But as it turned out, my mother, as my father had always been, was right.

Specifically, one evening, I had been watching a sports news program that was being broadcast on one of this nation's popular cable networks. This program reported that many of our professional baseball organizations were building training facilities in places such as the Dominican Republic, and were currently in the process of actively recruiting talent there. After watching this show, I now cringe every time I hear Joe Buck, while announcing the weekly baseball game, say, "And they did it with 'homegrown' talent."

Why then, with so much talent here within the United States, would these baseball organizations look for talent elsewhere? Well, it is their contention that fans, such as me, are "unwilling" to pay upward of $80 to watch the game. Due to my unwillingness and in hopes of getting me to open up my wallet, baseball owners are then "forced" to obtain the services of foreign ball players they say can be gotten at a more reasonable salary.

They will also have you believe that it's working and that the numbers, as the old saying goes, don't lie. In fact, during this same television show, a fellow Yankee fan had indicated that for the first time in his life, he was giving up his season tickets. Apparently, although he was in a financial position to afford it, he refused to pay $2,500 per seat per game. So I have to agree with the baseball owners. Their employment of foreign players will indeed not only have me opening my wallet, but they shall soon have me standing in line at the local bank in order to obtain a small business loan so that I will be able to watch that great American ballplayer Hideki Matsui.

Despite what those who hire illegal immigrants will tell you, these arguments hold water. It does not, however, give those who have allowed their pride to deny them employment the right to simply sit upon their ass and do nothing but complain.

As you can see from the foregoing, the gap in opinion between those who employ illegal immigrants and the American wage earner is as wide if not wider than the opinion of the Christian and atheist when it comes to the discussion of the existence of God. When it comes to the discussion of God, it is my belief there is no right or wrong; however, I believe the same cannot be said with regard to the employment of illegal immigrants. Accordingly, I want to remind those who do, that no matter what shade of color you want to paint your misconduct, there ain't no right way to do the wrong thing.

CHAPTER V

And in This Corner, Weighing In At...

(Everything That Glitters Is Not Gold)

You can fool some of the people all of the time, and all of people some of the time, but you cannot fool all of the people all of the time.
Abraham Lincoln, U.S. president

IN EVERY SPORTING EVENT, WITH THE EXCEPTION OF THOSE PER-taining to golf and bowling, that I have either attended or have watched on television, the opposing sides were outfitted in different colored uniforms. The reason for such should be obvious, but if it's not, they are outfitted in a way so that the fans, the players themselves, as well as those officiating the game are able to tell one team from another. Football has taken this step further by assigning numbers to certain positions in order to assist those officiating the game.

In the sport of boxing, there really isn't a need to utilize uniforms as it is an individual sport rather than a team sport. In some cases, the average fan is able to decipher who from whom simply by the color of their skin. But as we all know, that is more the exception than the rule. To further assist the average boxing fan who may be watching the fight on television and whose knowledge is limited to the names of the individuals fighting, the network televising the fight places the names of the boxers at the bottom of the screen followed by the color of the trunks they are wearing.

In the sports of golf and bowling, there is no regulation that I am aware of where the competitors are required to wear different clothing. In fact, if one so chooses, he or she could wear street clothes, and unless the person watching is an avid fan and knows what either the golfer or bowler physically looks like, I would venture to guess that if the athlete were to be standing next to a spectator, the average sporting fan would be unable to tell the athlete from the fan. Unless, of course, they were to look at their footwear.

At this juncture, you may be wondering what sports have to do with the issue of illegal immigration. Well, in every sport, you have at least two teams competing. When it comes to illegal immigration, you have those who are for it, while others oppose it. If illegal immigration were to be considered a sport, it would parallel golf and bowling, but be in direct opposition to the sport of football, when it comes to telling who from whom. Unless someone such as myself openly expresses their opinion as to which side of the issue they are on, there really isn't any ironclad way to tell which, if you'll pardon the analogy, team they are on.

In golf and/or bowling, there are commonly more than two teams or individuals competing at one time. Illegal immigration is no different. In the "game" of illegal immigration, there is a third team—those who say they are opposed to the issue yet act in direct opposition to what they say. My employer is one such individual. This is undoubtedly the team I fear the most.

In my opinion, these individuals or teams place the almighty dollar over what's in the best interests of this nation, and in doing so, they possibly compromise our nation's security. Moreover, while I cannot in good faith say that the actions of these individuals or teams are premeditated, they are, in my opinion, nothing more than wolves in sheep's clothing.

The following, in no particular order, is a partial list of those individuals and/or organizations who I believe, despite what they will have you believe, are PRO illegal immigration:

The American Civil Liberties Union (ACLU)

By its name alone, one would think this organization is solely for the protection of Americans' civil liberties, hence the word American in its title. If you thought that, you'd be both wrong and wronged. It is my understanding that this organization selects those cases or causes that would have the greatest impact upon our civil liberties.

For example, had this organization been around during the days of slavery, they would have you believe they would have filed suit on the behalf of those black Americans who, let's say for argument's sake, were denied the use of a white man's bathroom. That statement may have been true upon ACLU's inception, but I'm here to tell you that this is no longer the case when it comes to this organization.

Case in point: Approximately ten years ago, I sought the assistance of this organization with regard to a pending child-support case. In that I have a legal background, I didn't just send a letter whining about my situation, but along with the letter, I sent a verbatim transcript of my child-support hearing and included Xeroxed copies of case law that I believed supported my request.

Approximately one month after the submission of my request, I received in the U.S. mail a response indicating that the ACLU was unable to take on my case. While I'm not suggesting that my request was denied on the basis that I'm white, I believe it was denied because the wrongful taking of money from a divorced American without due process isn't high upon its list of things to do. Recent cases taken on by this organization have indeed shown its true colors.

Recently, a Southern California chapter of this organization filed suit against the Los Angeles Police Department for simply doing what they get paid to do—their job. Apparently, a motor vehicle that was being operated by an unlicensed, uninsured illegal immigrant was impounded for a period of 30 days pursuant to the appropriate vehicle code. It was my understanding that this organization argued that the illegal immigrant's constitutional rights were violated when his or her property was taken without due process.

In yet another unrelated case, the San Diego chapter of this organization filed suit against the City of Vista, California, when an American filed a Freedom of Information Act (FOIA) request for the names and companies who had filed permits to hire immigrants who stand on street corners looking for work. The ACLU, in this case, felt that the dissemination of this information was in violation of not only those filing for the permits but of those illegal immigrants looking for employment privacy. At the time of this writing, I am unaware of the court ruling in this case; what I do know is that the presiding judge gave this organization additional time to show cause as to why he should grant their request.

Because of this organization, the City of Escondido, California, was stopped from enforcing a city ordinance that prohibits landlords from renting to illegal immigrants. This organization argued that this ordinance was not only in violation of the illegal immigrants' constitutional rights, but they were being discriminated against solely because of their illegal status.

In my opinion, illegal immigration keeps this organization in business. Although they are a "nonprofit" organization, I wouldn't be surprised in the least bit if it is currently being funded by foreign governments.

Walmart (America's Favorite Superstore)

If what I am about to say is true, and I truly believe it is, Sam Walton, the founder of this superstore, shall soon, if he has not already, be turning in his grave. Now, I'm not suggesting that Walmart has a written or unwritten policy of hiring illegal immigrants; I am, however, suggesting that they have no problem whatsoever taking their money.

I do not have the statistics to prove this, but if I had to make an educated guess, I would say that at least six out of every ten products they sell is produced outside of the United States. In other words, Walmart takes money from individuals who are here illegally and then ships that money abroad in exchange for more items to sell. Yet, in the same breath, they pride themselves on supporting not only our troops, but their local communities as well.

If they truly supported our community, they would buy and sell more products that were made in the United States than those that were produced abroad. Moreover, instead of hiring retired Americans as greeters, they would instead hire INS agents.

I do, however, know of one company owned by an individual who is near and dear to my heart whose products are sold by this organization. Although I have never used any of its products, I can honestly say that the cosmetics made by Panco are made by Americans or those who are legally entitled to work here. Therefore, if you still feel a need to shop at Walmart after reading this book, I would highly recommend that if you're in the market for cosmetics, you consider purchasing Panco's line first.

The Entire Printing Industry

This is the industry that has barely put food on my table for over the past fourteen years. What I'm about to disclose to the reader about this industry is like Calgon's ancient Chinese secret when it comes to doing laundry.

The printing industry is, with the exception of maybe landscaping, one of the easiest professions to learn. In fact, many jobs within this industry require less skill than tying one's shoes in the morning. It is, therefore, my belief that many illegal immigrants seek out this industry for employment shortly after their unlawful entry into this country.

Also, this industry not only employs illegal immigrants, but has made and will continue to make millions because of them. The kicker is they do so "legally." As long as those illegally here continue to give birth to children, schools as well as other local government agencies must provide their parents with information. Since these children's parents neither read nor comprehend English, the information must then be disseminated in another language, either on the reverse side of the document or in another document altogether.

In general, printers take several things into account when quoting and subsequently billing out for their services. These things include but are not limited to cost of material (paper and ink), labor, and most importantly the number of impressions. So when an organization such as a school district, which educates children from illegal immigrants, needs to send out a flier, one side is normally printed in English, while the reverse is printed in another predominant language, most likely Spanish. Thus, the number of impressions increase; therefore, the respective printer then can charge more for its services.

For those reading this who have sometime in the past received such a flier and thought to themselves that the school or government agency was saving us money because they chose to print it two-sided rather than disseminating two pieces of correspondence, you need to think again. The only real savings would be in printing the correspondence in English only.

Unfortunately, school districts and government entities are not the only ones paying higher printing costs because of the illegal immigrant. Many other companies and organizations are now pretty much forced to do the same when it comes to the marketing of their services or products.

As the reader can see, this industry stands to lose tens of thousands, if not millions, of dollars should any law be passed ridding ourselves of illegal immigration.

Social Security Administration

Speaking of a sinking ship, it is public knowledge that this administration is in deep financial trouble. It's in trouble simply because those who are drawing upon it have, in the past, paid less into it than what they are currently receiving from it. Several presidents, politicians, as well as economists, have attempted to right the ship. However, all who have tried have failed.

At first, I was of the belief that the Social Security Administration was using the illegal immigration issue as a temporary "band-aid." Specifically, I've often wondered what happened to the money that was sent into this administration by those who employ illegal immigrants that didn't match up to the alleged Social Security number the money was sent under. In fact, I honestly believed that the Social Security Administration turned its head and subsequently applied that money to other accounts in hopes of a bailout.

Recently, I have been led to believe that my assumption of the above is incorrect and I shall describe this elsewhere in this book. Despite this, I have included this administration in this chapter in the event the information I received from the local newspaper on this subject is incorrect.

Rush Limbaugh and the Likes of Him

It is from his loyal listeners that I believe I will receive the most opposition as to the content of this chapter. Some, most likely hundreds of thousands of Americans, are liable to accuse me of defaming an American icon.

I'm not, and to be quite honest, this man, in my opinion, is not an American icon. Rather, he is nothing more than a self-proclaimed windbag who claims to reside, along with his formerly nicotine-stained fingertips, in a cave he refers to as the EIB network, somewhere within New York or Florida. He makes millions because of the illegal immigration issue as well as other controversial topics.

Some will even go so far as to say he is an American hero. I'm not one of those. He's interesting, to say the least, but no hero. He's a man with the talent of gab and very low self-esteem. Despite being one of the best orators I have ever heard, he, without a doubt, promotes what he says he clearly wants to eradicate.

Here is a man, so much like me, with an opinion on everything. He openly criticizes those who are currently in office or running for one, while he himself hasn't stepped up to the plate. I first thought he lacked the intestinal fortitude, then I realized that wasn't it at all. Why would a man, who I believe earns a seven-digit yearly income, give up his job for one that pays no more than $200,000 a year? I'm confident that if he were to run for the office of president, I don't think he would win, or at least I hope he wouldn't. I do, however, believe he would indeed be a force to be reckoned with.

Nevertheless, what concerns me most about this man and his microphone is that he has misdirected all the attention upon himself, when such attention should be directed toward those issues currently affecting this nation. Instead of expressing their opinions on hot topics such as illegal immigration to those who make the laws, his loyal listeners are content with calling his network, waiting for minutes, if not hours, for the chance to speak with him or just to hear themselves on the radio.

If these "loyal" listeners put forth as much effort reducing their views to writing and sending them off to their congressmen or better yet taking time out to vote into office those individuals who agree with their respective views, we just might be able to rid ourselves of this rapidly growing problem. In other words, a decrease in his salary, as well as others', will surely be a sign that the problem of illegal immigration is diminishing.

Some may feel by my calling out the aforementioned individuals and organizations that I have, in a sense, unfairly and without any provocation on their part, thrown and subsequently landed the ultimate "sucker" punch.

Despite not being one to fight in accordance with the Marquess of Queensberry rules, I shall upon publication provide each individual and organization called out a copy of this book in order, if they so choose, to rebut anything that I have written about them.

Some may also feel that I am a hypocrite for indicating that someone other than myself lacked the intestinal fortitude to run for public office. I agree in part.

In my case, it isn't necessarily the lack of intestinal fortitude that stops me from running for the office of the president of the United States, rather it's the lack of capital. That's right, the public education system has failed to teach us that along with being 35 years of age and a natural-born citizen, one needs to possess a pair of pants with extremely deep pockets. Unfortunately for me, my pockets at the moment are sewn shut.

Even had I possessed the capital, it's doubtful that anyone with morals would support a man such as myself, who openly admits that he possesses a criminal record, admits to paying for sex, has inhaled on more than one occasion, and has in the past failed to pay his taxes. However, I can proudly stand before the American public and honestly say that at no time in my life have I ever employed, with or without knowledge, an illegal immigrant to either clean my home or watch my children.

While I cannot speak on the behalf of others, as for me, I have come to realize that everything that glitters is not gold.

CHAPTER VI

Until Death Do Us Part
(Or at Least Until I Get My Green Card)

Marriage is not a noun. It's a verb. It isn't something you get. It's something you do. It's the way you love your partner every day.
Barbara De Angelis, author

AT BEST, I CAN BE DESCRIBED AS A MAN WHO IS ALONE, BUT NOT lonely. I am one who greatly misses being in a relationship, yet unwilling to enter into one simply for the sake of saying I'm in one.

It is evident that, based upon the current high rate of divorce, many Americans are not of this same belief. Not only are Americans entering into relationships for "bragging rights," but recently I was apprised of a man who asked for a woman's hand in marriage for the sole purpose of securing a home for both him and his son.

After hearing of this man's plight, I had thought to myself that entering into a relationship for solely obtaining a place to live was, in my opinion, the height of stupidity. It did, however, have me reflecting upon my own life and, as my first marriage will attest, that I, too, have entered into a relationship for the wrong reason.

In December 1978, while stationed aboard Marine Corps Air Station, Tustin, California, I met my first wife, Shirley. As she tells it, she was sitting on my roommate's rack (bed) while waiting for him to finish showering before an evening out on the town. Apparently, after a six-hour plane flight coupled with a ninety-minute cab ride home from the airport, I was completely inebriated. So much so, I was unable to unlock my barracks room door and ended up climbing through a window.

She also told me that before passing out on my bed, I had informed her that at some point in the future, I was going to marry her. Although she had been dating my roommate, Jeff, at the time, that relationship, for whatever reason, ended and Shirley and I began to date.

As with many other budding relationships, we too had our share of problems, which ultimately led to our breakup. At some point after our breakup, Shirley began to date her superior noncommissioned officer (boss). She was not only a cheerleader for my squadron, but a Marine herself who had been assigned to the base communications squadron. With the exception of seeing her at the sporting events in which I participated, I had very little contact with her subsequent to our breakup.

One day, out of the clear blue sky, Shirley came into my office in tears. After seeing how distraught she was, I asked her what was wrong and, if there was something indeed wrong, what, if anything, could I do to help her. After several minutes of tears, she was able to catch her breath long enough to inform me that she was four months pregnant.

I need not tell the male reader what went through my mind at that moment. However, any thought I might have had along that line was immediately removed when she informed me that I was not the father of her unborn child. At that point, I wasn't clear as to whether the tears she had shed were out of joy or for some other reason. That too became very clear.

It seemed that her superior noncommissioned officer was not only the father of her unborn child, but, as I soon discovered, he was also married. After finding out the results of her pregnancy test, she approached the father of the child. Upon receiving this news, this man quickly informed her that he and his wife had decided to reconcile and would be soon relocating to Hawaii.

Now being aware of her predicament and being unsure of her position on it, I informed her that I felt that her best course of action would be to have the child aborted. Upon hearing her statement "that all men are the same," I assumed that I was not the only man in her life who had recently given her that advice. Since she told me she was adamantly opposed to abortion and based upon the fact the she felt the father of her unborn child should be held accountable for his actions, I informed her that as an alternative, she could, if she so chose, report her pregnancy to the father's superior officer.

For those of you who are not familiar with military law, adultery at that time was, and may very well still be, against the law. Being well aware of the fact that the father of her unborn child could possibly lose his career, and still very emotionally attached, Shirley decided against this course of action.

At some point after that, the father of her unborn child and his wife relocated to Hawaii, while Shirley and I ended up rekindling our previous short-lived relationship. As her due date approached and since things were going well between us, I decided to ask for her hand in marriage, a proposal that she accepted. When I proposed to her, I honestly believed that I was not only doing it out of the love I had for her, but I also felt her unborn child deserved a "father."

In November 1979, after losing $1,000 (it seems I was running bad at the poker table), Shirley and I were married in the Chapel of the Roses, which was located in Las Vegas,

Nevada. The morning afterward and after spending our last $135 on our wedding, I, along with my new bride, returned home. Upon our return, we both filed the appropriate paperwork with our respective units in order for us to obtain permission to live off base.

Shortly after obtaining this approval, we rented an apartment in the city of Santa Ana. One evening, I had been awakened by the moans of discomfort emitting from Shirley, and a very damp bed. Apparently, she felt that if she wasn't going to get a good night's rest, neither was I.

After we both came to the conclusion that her water broke and her labor process had just begun, I got up and headed toward the shower. On my way to the shower, I asked her if she wouldn't mind ironing me a shirt. Subsequent to my brief shower, I, along with my newly pressed shirt and my wife, who had been in labor for some time, got into our car and headed toward the Naval Hospital in Long Beach.

During the ride to the hospital, the baby's head began to crown, so it only stood to reason that Shirley would be giving birth to "our" daughter, Michelle, within minutes of our arrival. Immediately upon her birth, Michelle was diagnosed with some sort of unknown respiratory problem. Approximately three days after Michelle's birth, Shirley was discharged from the hospital and returned home without our child.

The day following her return home, Shirley received a call from the Naval Hospital indicating that Michelle had just been transported to Children's Hospital, also located in Long Beach, for further tests and treatment as deemed necessary. Sadly, approximately two weeks after her transfer to Children's Hospital, Michelle passed away. It seems that the respiratory problem was the result of being born with half of a heart.

After Michelle's burial, Shirley and I attempted the best we could to get on with our lives. In fact, I was promoted and received a transfer to the 8th Marine Corps Recruiting District, located in New Orleans, Louisiana. Shirley, who was by then honorably discharged from the Marine Corps, found a wonderful paying opportunity with Western Union.

It wasn't long after this that I realized that neither of us was in love; rather, we got married in order that our daughter, Michelle, had both a mother and a father. I came to this conclusion upon my return home to an empty house on one Christmas Eve.

As you can see, I clearly am in no position to pass judgment upon someone who was willing to enter into a relationship for nothing more than a residence. In fact, my actions validate the statement that "those who live in glass houses should not throw stones." Moreover, getting married for the reason I did is much like the employer who pays an American poorly with little or no benefits. Specifically, doing so is not unlawful; it is, however, in my opinion, poor business practice. My marriage to Shirley was nothing less than a crime against the heart.

Even to a man who is of little or no faith, some things are sacred. In my very humble opinion, marriage and committed relationships fall within that realm. No one or anything for whatever reason should be allowed to purposely tarnish them.

But just like my belief that no one should enter a relationship for the sake of saying they are in one, this opinion is also not shared by the majority. In fact, many illegal immigrants have tarnished the institution of marriage solely for the purpose of obtaining nothing more than an American citizenship. In doing so, they are breaking the law, just as the employer does who hires them.

In order to perpetrate his or her crime, the illegal immigrant, in so many words, recruits the assistance of an American, who is not only willing to break the law, but is willing to give up a portion of his or her life.

I currently work with such an individual. Jerome (last name withheld for obvious reasons) is a man who gets paid less than I do and therefore has no "pot to piss in," let alone a window to throw it out of.

Jerome, as he has told me, met Muriel while he was living with and attending to the medical needs of his elderly mother. Muriel lived next door to "Jerry," the name he is referred to by his mother, who, herself, was attending to the needs of an elderly relative. They struck up a mutual friendship and ended up talking for several hours a day.

At some point during one of these conversations, Muriel had the occasion to mention to Jerome that she was in this country on a temporary visa. Apparently, the visa that she was on was either nearing its end or she would have to return to her country in the event the care she was providing was no longer needed.

One day, after reporting for work, Jerome approached one of the owners of our company for the purpose of obtaining approval for the following day off. The owner had told me before granting this request that he had inquired into the specific reason why Jerome needed the day off. He told me that Jerome had said he needed the time off to get married. Since Jerome had neither spoken of nor ever been seen with any woman, the owner asked him as to why he was getting married. I'm told Jerome indicated it was because he and his future bride were sexually compatible.

After receiving the approval, Jerome and Muriel were married in the City of San Diego before the justice of the peace, or maybe "justice of the piece" is more appropriate in this case.

Nevertheless, it wasn't until a month or so after this blessed event had transpired—when I had asked Jerome why he was taking so much time off work, knowing he wouldn't be paid—that he admitted to me that he had gotten married. Despite already being aware that he had gotten married, I was blown away. Here was a man who not only was living with his mother but was getting underpaid as if he, himself, was an illegal immigrant.

Inquiring minds, such as mine, wanted to know why a man in his predicament would even remotely consider taking on a wife. So I asked him as to why he had gotten married, and I too was told it was because he and his bride were sexually compatible.

After hearing this, I honestly thought that he was asking for the time off so he could satisfy his sexual needs with his bride. In fact, I thought to myself that this woman was so great in bed that he not only felt a need to marry her, but he was willing to go halfway around the world to be with her.

Half jokingly, I told him what I had been thinking, and after hearing what I had to say, he then told me that the reason he needed so much time off was not to satisfy his sexual desires, but to obtain a green card for his new bride.

During the next couple of months, Jerome and I spent a considerable amount of time together, as he was not only my co-worker, but he was also the frontman of our now defunct rock band, Checkered Past. On several occasions, not only did he explain the process of getting a green card, but often expressed his frustration with the system. Because of these talks, it is now my understanding that obtaining a green card is not as simple as filling out forms and paying the appropriate fees.

In fact, he led me to believe that in addition to filling out the appropriate forms and paying the fees, in order to "consummate" their green card, they had to remain married for a certain amount of time and maintain a joint residence. He also said that he was required to fill out and sign a statement of responsibility. Apparently, by doing so, he was acknowledging that he was not only financially responsible for Muriel, but legally responsible for all of her actions as well. Moreover, he stated that both he and Muriel were questioned, both jointly and separately, by a panel of government officials.

Although he didn't say, I assume the government panel does so to ensure that the marriage is more than simply a paper drill in order to obtain a green card. He also made no mention as to whether or not he could dissolve the marriage.

I have to assume when it comes to the dissolution of the marriage, if it occurs after the prescribed time, the individual in possession of the green card would be allowed to stay here. In the event the marriage was dissolved prior to the time prescribed, I would guess that the individual's green card would be withdrawn and that person be ordered back to his or her country of origin.

Getting back on point, I have to admit that being sexually compatible with your partner is a key to a successful relationship. It's important, but it's not the only thing, and in my opinion, is certainly not a reason to get married. If the truth be told, the older I get, the more I'm finding out that conversation over a cup of coffee with someone you like is, at times, as much or more of a turn-on than a quick roll around in the hay.

Jerome's excuse to get married had also reminded me of a conversation I once had with a woman whom I, at some point in my life, casually dated. It was her opinion that sex, while it was both pleasurable and somewhat important, played a very small role in her daily life. Not only did this statement put me on the defensive, but I honestly thought I was receiving the "birds and the bees" talk from Mother Superior.

Her next statement, however, spoke volumes. She continued to tell me that no matter how much you enjoy sex with your partner, in all reality, you spend more time out of bed than you do in it with them. In other words, if being sexually compatible is the only thing you have in common, you are going to be unhappy more than happy.

Nevertheless, I'm a man, and so very much like the next man, I indeed enjoy sex. In fact, I'm willing to talk about it at the drop of a hat. During my sexual career, I have experienced bad sex, good sex, great sex, and with one woman in particular (Susan gets honorable mention here), sex that was, in my opinion, off the charts. Although I have on occasion told a woman that I would do just about anything to have sex with her again, I can honestly say marriage had never entered my mind.

That being said, I wanted to hear a description of the sex that had a man willing to marry for it. At the risk of not sounding crude, I must say my first thought was that Muriel's vagina was made of platinum, trimmed in the finest of gold. So I asked and after hearing Jerome's response, I now know why attorneys never ask a question that they do not already know the answer to.

Not only was I not prepared for his answer, but it, to say the least, floored me. He informed me that he had never had sex with Muriel and also felt that even if he had wanted to, her physical appearance didn't appeal to him. So much so that he doubted he would be able to maintain an erection in order to have sex.

After hearing this admission, I then asked why he chose to lie to everyone regarding his rationale for getting married. He told me that he had to come up with a reason other than obtaining a green card and being sexually compatible was the only reason he could think of at the moment.

Needless to say, my opinion of him changed drastically. In fact, I thought that any man willing to give up any portion of his life for the benefit of another surely possessed a heart the size of the state of Texas. But that opinion was short-lived. I, then, after considering all the circumstances of his case, found him not to be a man who possessed a very large heart; rather, he was now nothing more than a common criminal.

I guess at this juncture, based upon the fact that he has yet to get caught, it would be premature for me to label him a criminal. However, if at some point he is caught and subsequently convicted, I would then label him a very inept criminal. Maybe with the exception of someone possibly arranging for the payment and sale of an illegal drug, I can't imagine anyone committing a crime that does not in some way benefit him or herself.

Except for receiving a little more money back on his income tax return, he received no benefit for his "crime." In other words, doing what he did is like a person holding up a bank and, instead of demanding money, he attempted to make a deposit by force.

At this point, I am unsure if the marriage is even legal. I have always heard the phrase, "consummate the marriage," but I am not sure what relevance it really has. If one fails to consummate one's marriage, does it mean they are not married? It could very well mean that they are indeed married in the eyes of the law, but not so in the eyes of what they consider their Higher Power.

Since I have not spoken to Jerome in months, he and Muriel may have since consummated her green card. I have, however, been apprised that both he and Muriel still maintain separate residences, which in itself is a violation of the conditions of her green card. If caught, Jerome might want to consider using the "I didn't consummate the green card" defense.

Setting aside all my feelings with regard to the subject of illegal immigration, I must admit that I am not without compassion for someone who is in Muriel's position. In fact, and in lieu of a better word, I too was almost "trapped" into marriage for the sole purpose of obtaining a green card for another.

Approximately one year after the death of my first love, Tiffany Kinner, and during my grieving process, I sought out a prospective partner via a biker dating site on the Internet. Out of the many responses I received after placing the ad, I answered but one. In fact, it was the only one that had caught my eye.

It is here where Claudia (last name withheld for reasons that should shortly become apparent) came into my life. After exchanging several emails, she at some point suggested that we talk on the telephone. After about a week of these telephone conversations, we mutually agreed that it was time to take the relationship to the next level by arranging to meet in person over a cup of coffee.

Up until this point, I had no clue as to what she physically looked like. I can tell you that the image I formed in my mind was one of an American of Italian descent. This image that I had formed was based upon her last name and the fact that she spoke fluent but broken English. After setting my eyes upon her for the very first time, I realized that my name was nowhere near The Amazing Kreskin.

Her beauty, to say the least, had left me breathless. With the exception of Susan, Tiffany, and Rebecca, I can honestly say that she was by far the prettiest woman I had ever had the pleasure of dating. Shortly after catching my breath, I soon discovered that she was not an American but had been born to Italian parents and raised in the country of Argentina. Getting the rest of first-date questions out of the way, we ended our date and went our separate ways.

Approximately two days later, and since the first date appeared to have gone well, we decided to meet again. This time, it was going to be over dinner and a drink. This date did not, however, go as well as the first, and as it turned out, it was the beginning of the demise of our relationship. It seems that at some point during the date, the conversation got around to the topic of illegal immigration.

Although I cannot recall the specifics of the conversation, I do recall that I was no longer the invisible man having dinner with his date. In fact, everyone in the restaurant, including the busboy with the gold tooth, had been hanging on each and every word that had emitted from my mouth. At the time, I remember feeling like I was a broker for EF Hutton.

Needless to say, the date ended immediately after dinner. Before getting into her vehicle and driving away, Claudia opened up the trunk to her car and pulled out what appeared to be a black wooden box. In this box, as I soon discovered, among other important papers, was her work visa. Apparently, and rightfully so, she felt that if she was ever going to see me again, she had to prove she was in this country legally.

We continued to date for approximately six months after this awkward evening. As time went on, I became more and more uncomfortable with the relationship. It seemed that, with the exception of those with whom she worked, the majority of her friends were in this country illegally.

On occasion, Claudia held gatherings at her home, which many of these same illegal immigrants attended. Not only did the appearance of these individuals make me feel uncomfortable, but I didn't know whether to leave or just call the INS.

Because of her guest list, I ended up attending fewer and fewer of these gatherings. If by chance I was going to see her on the day of one of these gatherings, I would time my arrival so that the gathering was almost over.

It wasn't long after the last gathering I had attended sometime in November, that Claudia's work visa became an issue. I'm not sure where we were at the time, but she chose to tell me that her ten-year work visa was due to expire the following May. Not knowing anything about visas, I then asked her why she had not made an attempt to renew it. Seemed to me that seven months was ample enough time to do so. She indicated that she had made an attempt to renew it, but was told it would not be renewed.

Well, this acknowledgment pretty much ended the relationship for me. Although she told me that it was not the case, I felt as if she was only on that dating site in order to attach herself to a "host" for the sole purpose of obtaining a green card for both herself and her two children. Before she could get out any further explanation, I quickly pointed out that, unlike my friend Jerome, I was not an individual who was willing to marry for the sole purpose of obtaining a green card for another.

The relationship ended approximately three weekends afterward. We were to have spent the weekend together, but on Saturday evening, after dinner and while I was sitting on the couch watching television, she informed me that she had something to tell me and wasn't sure as to how I was going to receive it. She then proceeded to tell me that since I was unwilling to marry her, a friend of hers was willing to do so. She also wanted me to know that she was not doing this for her own benefit, but for the possibility of a better life for her children.

She did, however, indicate that despite being married to another man, she had the desire to continue dating with the possibility of marriage farther down the road. She received her answer when I put on my shoes, grabbed my belongings and left. With the exception of a few brief emails and one telephone call after my departure, I have not had any further contact with her.

I guess it would be reasonable for someone to ask why a man like me would have any compassion for a woman who I had thought was dating me for nothing more than a green card. Moreover, it would be less reasonable for a man that possesses the view toward illegal immigration as I do to have any compassion whatsoever. But I do.

Here is a woman who first came to this country for a vacation in 1993. As many others like her did, she saw the possibility of a better life for her and her family. So upon her return to Argentina, both she and her husband applied for and were granted a work visa into the United States.

Shortly after their arrival and for reasons unbeknownst to me, Claudia and her husband were divorced. After her divorce, Claudia then began dating an American and ultimately ended up marrying him. Although she and I had never talked in detail about this marriage, she did mention that it was for a reason other than obtaining a green card. In fact, she made it a point to tell me that this man had offered to file the appropriate paperwork on her behalf in order to obtain a green card and that she had declined such an offer. She told me she had done so because she felt she could not only obtain it through her own efforts, but she wanted to.

As the story goes, this man did not file the papers on her behalf and that marriage was soon dissolved. I assume she was banking upon the fact that her visa would be renewed without her husband's assistance.

As we know, all of us at some point in our lives are faced with making decisions. Claudia was no exception. I have to assume that before making the decision to relocate herself and her family, she did so knowing that the possibility existed that her visa would not be renewed and she would then be asked to return to Argentina. It was also her choice to decline her American husband's offer to file paperwork for the said green card on her behalf. That decision, while both noble and understandable, as it turns out was her last chance at American citizenship.

It is here where I have all the compassion in the world for her. Who can blame a woman who saw an opportunity for a better life that in the end did not pan out? Moreover, here is a woman who has invested ten years of her life busting her ass to provide for herself and for her children, without any assistance from the United States government. She also told me, although I can't verify this, that she paid taxes during this period. Additionally, she told me it would be unfair that the

United States would then ask her to leave after all that she has done. In her opinion, everything she has worked so hard for in the past ten years or so would all be for naught, and I agree.

I cannot speak for others, nor will I attempt to do so here; however, I will admit that I have personally made several decisions throughout my lifetime that quite frankly did not turn out as I had hoped. For those that did, I have reaped the benefits, and for those that didn't I have and may continue to suffer their consequences.

It is here where I must now get down from the compassion wagon and climb aboard the reality wagon. Whether or not I feel Claudia got the short end of the stick, so to speak, is irrelevant. Should she now decide to extend her stay within the United States of America beyond the expiration of her visa and without the government's permission to do so, then she is breaking the law. Should she indeed choose this course of action, then, in my opinion, she is no better than any other illegal immigrant.

May has since come and gone, and as I have not had any contact with her, I assume she is either living in this country illegally or decided to do the right thing by returning to her native country of Argentina. Either way, I sincerely wish her the best.

Despite those reasons for getting married that I have set forth above, and notwithstanding the fact that it has taken me almost a half century to learn this lesson, I believe there is but one reason to get married. In fact, I can honestly say that I have experienced this reason only twice in my life, and both times were with a woman who was not my wife.

That one thing is love. I would venture a guess that a good many of you who are reading this book are of the belief that two times is a very low number. While I might agree with that, I must admit that I twice have experienced something that many have spent their entire lives looking for and never experiencing it.

Unfortunately, my first love ended in tragedy. Tiffany was a woman more than ten years my junior whose looks could at worst be classified as stunning and, despite what some others might have thought, was even more beautiful on the inside.

As with many of us, one evening she made a very poor decision, and that decision took her life. Her death, while tragic, was not in vain. This woman not only touched my heart in places I never knew existed, but she is the one who taught this "old" man that in order to be loved, one must love himself first. Moreover, her death was the catalyst for the friendship I value dearly with her mother, Barbara, who despite her own loss, through her teachings and her compassion, made sense of her daughter's death for me. I am not only grateful, but believe it is the most unselfish act I have ever witnessed.

Her death also made way for the only other love of my life, Susan, who was equally, if not more, as stunning as Tiffany and possessed everything a man could ever want in a partner, and then some. By then some, I mean that she not only had a husband, but had been living with another man for at least the last five years.

Although I can honestly say that at the beginning, I was unaware of her unavailability status, in fairness to her, she soon made it known to me and I proceeded forward with my intentions nevertheless. Honestly, I thought that this would end up being nothing more than the proverbial "one-night stand."

Not only did I not know that this would end up being the greatest sexual experience of my life, but just as Elvin Bishop did during the 1970s, I fooled around and ended up falling in love. Despite the fact that there is nothing more in this world that I want more than a committed relationship with her, she ended it like an episode from "Seinfeld." She said she wanted out because she could no longer lead a double, or shall I say triple, life and that the breakup wasn't because of me, it was because of her.

If anything, I have learned two things from the time I spent with Susan: One should have the conviction to end one relationship before starting another and, more importantly, it was never the one I could live with that I desired, it's the one I can't live without.

With the exception of the birth of my two children, Andrew Todd and Nicholas Charles, the experiences I have had with each of these women have been the greatest experiences of my life. I would not trade them for anything and, just like my dreams, no one or entity can ever take those experiences away from me.

Allowing illegal immigrants to marry solely on the hope of someday becoming a citizen is not only criminal, but it is rapidly tarnishing the institution of marriage. Our failure as a nation to prevent this is so much like the cook who keeps adding water to the soup until it becomes tasteless.

Should we allow this misconduct to continue, it shall not be long before the marriage license that many of us have paid for and cherish will be reduced to nothing more than an expensive piece of toilet paper.

CHAPTER VII

Anchors Aweigh

(We're Gonna Make It So You Won't Send Us Home)

Home is the place where boys and girls first learn how to limit their wishes, abide by rules, and consider the rights and needs of others.
Sidonie Gruenberg, American educator and author

WHEN I INITIALLY SAT DOWN TO WRITE THIS BOOK, I HAD NO IN-tention whatsoever of writing this chapter, not because I didn't think it had any relevance, but because it has always been my belief that children, for the most part, are innocent.

Although I have not wavered in that opinion, I now be-lieve that the offspring of those immigrants who are here il-legally, through no fault of their own, pose a grave danger to this nation. As we all know, and much to my dismay, the United States Constitution as currently amended gives citi-zenship to individuals based solely upon the fact that they were born upon our soil or the soil of one of our possessions.

So when it comes around to the subject of the deportation of those illegally here, there are many in this nation who be-lieve that those illegal immigrants who have given birth to an American should not be deported. They feel it would not only be a violation of this "American's" constitutional rights to be forced, along with their illegal immigrant parents, to leave their country, but this "American" has an additional right to be raised by their birth parents upon our soil.

I couldn't disagree more. In fact, it is my contention that, in hopes of staying here, those illegal immigrants, who are not only aware of our laws but also of our compassion, are then encouraged to give birth to these "Americans."

In many cases, if not all, because many of these same illegal immigrants do not have enough insurance to cover the expense of the birth, we Americans end up paying for these births, and the illegal immigrants then turn around and apply and subsequently receive services from our government on behalf of their American child—services that many Americans are denied because they make too much.

However, receiving free medical treatment and services, although a drain upon our economy, is not the danger I am referring to. Allowing the illegal immigrant to remain and raise these Americans is.

I can honestly say that my parents have had, and will continue to have, the most influence upon my life. Apparently, my parents are not the only ones who have had influence over their children. I am reminded of an individual who had been assigned to my platoon in basic training. I cannot recall his first name, but his last name, if my memory serves me correctly, was Townsend. I believe he was no more than nineteen years of age and had enlisted in his home state of Tennessee, like many others, right out of high school.

Approximately halfway through our training, there was a change of command with regard to those who trained us. This is when Staff Sgt. Green, who at that time was considered by the Marine Corps to be a "dark green" Marine, came into my life. In this day and age, many of you would consider him to be an African-American.

The morning after his arrival, Staff Sgt. Green ordered our platoon out to the parade deck for formation, and all of us, with the exception of Pvt. Townsend, complied. As soon as it was discovered that he was missing, Staff Sgt. Green went back into the barracks looking for him.

It wasn't long until I heard Pvt. Townsend yell that he didn't take orders from a "nigger." To this day, I don't know what occurred immediately after that. I do, however, remember that whatever happened, it caused Pvt. Townsend to double-time toward the formation with a ripped blouse.

With the exception of disobeying an order from a superior noncommissioned officer, I felt as if Pvt. Townsend had done nothing wrong. I realize that by stating this, many of you are now thinking that my true colors have indeed shown through.

Believe that as you may, but in saying what I did, I am in no way condoning the fact that he had called Staff Sgt. Green a nigger. I am, however, saying that Pvt. Townsend only acted in the way that he had been brought up.

But just as I believe Pvt. Townsend was brought up improperly, I believe the offspring of the illegal immigrant will be brought up in a way that will eventually pose a threat to this nation. Should we allow those here illegally to stay and raise these Americans, they will do so with the language, values, beliefs, and traditions of the country that they left to come here illegally.

Herein lies the problem. When these Americans who have been raised upon the values of another country reach the age of majority, they will receive yet another right in accordance with the United States Constitution—the right to vote.

I assume these voters, as many of us did when we voted for the first time, will either vote for those individuals their parents tell them to vote for or, as an alternative, shall vote upon the values that have been instilled upon them since birth. Unfortunately, if these Americans vote enough people into office with their values, it soon won't be long before we as a nation are living under those values and not ours.

Many, if not all, of the illegal immigrants whom I have either worked with or met along the way are, in my opinion, far from stupid. This being the case, I'm now left to wonder, with the current state of our economy and the fact that they are grossly underpaid, why they would then willingly consider having a child.

It had also left me with yet another question—a question that will surely get the attention of this nation's conspiracy theorists. Did these immigrants come here to willfully have children in hopes of a better life for themselves or were they directed to do so by someone or something else?

I realize that what I am about to say is an extreme stretch, but is it possible that, just as Saddam Hussein found his way around the nuclear arms ban by producing biological weapons, countries, such as the one immediately to our south, have found a less combative way (giving birth to Americans and then raising them with their values) of taking back what they feel is rightfully theirs—our country?

Although I seriously doubt that this is the case, I will not, at this juncture, rule out that possibility.

Sadly, it seems that the Republicans want the illegal immigrants for cheap labor and the Democrats for their votes. Others such as I just want our country, as well as our jobs, back.

Chapter VIII

WIN

(What's Important Now)

Time is the coin of your life. It is the only coin you have, and only you can determine how it will be spent. Be careful lest you let other people spend it for you.
Carl Sandburg, American poet

AT THE TIME OF THIS WRITING, THIS NATION HAD BEEN IN THE process of electing a new president, a process this nation undergoes every four years. Being forty-nine years of age, it certainly was not my first election and, Invisible Man willing, hopefully it shall not be my last. It was, however, for whatever reason, the one that I had paid the closest attention to.

Despite the fact that it was not my first election, I don't want to leave the reader with the opinion that when it comes to politics, I possess the wisdom of Solomon. Sadly, nothing could be further from the truth. In fact, I am a man whose only indication, prior to this election, that this country might have been in a recession was based solely on the fact that his favorite local streetwalker charged more for oral sex.

So it was neither new nor surprising to me that several individuals were willing to stand before me and the entire American public to tell us not only what we wanted, but in the same breath, what was in our best interests as a nation. Up until this election, I always bought into their knowing the answers. However, now I started questioning how these candidates knew not only what I wanted, but what was in the best interests of this country.

I have to assume that since I had not received a letter, phone call or a visit from any of these candidates or a member of their staff, they must have either consulted a crystal ball or employed the services of a psychic. As I don't put much faith in either, I must have been out of the country when these candidates attempted to contact me.

According to my count, there were approximately eight individuals who ran for the office of the world's most important person. I use the word "person" here, as one woman ran for such office. Moreover, I have also chosen the word "important" instead of "powerful" because the only power this individual possesses upon being "appointed" president is the power of suggestion.

Quite frankly, I'm not sure why we make all this fuss over this one individual. It seems to me, we should be more concerned with the ideas of those who run for the office of Congress or Senate. After all, it is these individuals and not the president who make the laws that will determine our fate.

Nevertheless, out of the eight individuals who ran for office, there were four front-runners. In my opinion, none of those candidates addressed or provided an adequate solution to what I believe to be the most important issue currently facing this nation—illegal immigration.

In fact, one candidate had us believing that he deserved our vote because he served his country in the armed forces, and, while doing so, became a prisoner of war; one believed she deserved it because of her gender; another wanted our vote solely because of the color of his skin; and the remaining candidate wanted it so he could instill his family values upon us. In fairness to these individuals, they had also brought into light the issues and problems they intended to solve upon their appointment as the highest ranking American. Nevertheless, I was left with the opinion that what I have stated above was their biggest selling point.

I could not, however, in good faith cast my vote for either of the candidates who asked me to do so because of their gender or color of their skin. Essentially, they were asking me to do something they themselves would not like to have done to them. For example, neither of these two individuals would be at all too happy should they be denied something simply because of their gender or the color of their skin. They were, in effect, asking for their cake and wanting to eat it too.

The individual who wanted my vote in order to instill his family values also did not receive my vote. It seems as if the family values he wanted to instill were based upon his faith. While I have nothing against his faith, the First Amendment to the U.S. Constitution implies there should be a division of church and state. Moreover, as this man is faith driven, I was reminded of those countries in the Middle East where they, too, are faith driven. It seems to me that they are in constant war with each other.

The remaining candidate, based upon his service record, was, in my humble opinion, the individual who was most qualified out of the four to hold the office of the president of the United States. Despite my opinion, he too did not get my vote. It's not that I didn't think he deserved it or appreciate what he had done for this country, it's because I adamantly opposed his view on illegal immigration.

In that I didn't have a particular candidate to vote for in that election, I was left to look for answers elsewhere. It was during that search that I found what I believed to be the solution to all of the problems currently facing this nation. The answer, as I soon discovered, was an acronym that was used during a television interview, an interview that, believe it or not, was of someone other than those who had run for office. In fact, the person being interviewed, in the grand scheme of life, is known to most as nothing more than a football coach.

I felt as if the acronym spoke volumes. In fact, I thought so much of it, that I chose to use it as the title of this chapter.

Before being reduced to a television college football analyst, the person interviewed, Lou Holtz, got paid to win nothing more than a game, and based upon his record, a job he performed rather well. In fact, he will forever be known by many as one of the greatest coaches who has ever coached the game.

Unless I misunderstood him, I believe Mr. Holtz was attempting to tell those of us that were viewing, one must, in order to be successful, first identify his or her weaknesses and then "tackle," if you pardon the expression, the most important issue facing them at the moment.

Many Americans believe it is our economy that is the most important issue facing this nation at this moment. It's not! The reason why the economy is in the shape it is in is, in my opinion, of utmost importance. Unless we get to the root of the problem, the economy shall continue upon its current course, and therefore it won't be long before we as a nation are at the mercy of the rest of the world.

To prove my point, former President Bush, during the later part of his second term, sent out stimulus checks in hopes of stimulating the economy. Herein lies the problem. Without first eliminating the cause of our failing economy, which I believe to be illegal immigration, those who were out stimulating the economy with their checks found that, upon their return, their job was either shipped overseas or was currently being performed by an illegal immigrant.

Additionally, if my assumption is indeed correct that Lou Holtz is right, then, based upon the top two "newsworthy" stories that were broadcast on one of this nation's most popular news networks at the beginning of 2008, we as a nation are nowhere near identifying our weaknesses, much less "tackling" the most important issues facing us at the moment. In fact, we are in a whole lot of trouble.

According to this network, it seems our two most important issues of that day were about a baseball player who had allegedly used an illegal performance-enhancing drug and a congressman who had solicited another for a sexual favor. Other less important issues such as our failing economy were not broadcast until the completion of these two stories and the weather. I did, however, get a great deal of comfort knowing that while I and millions of other Americans are going broke, temperatures would be reaching the mid 80s with no chance of showers in the forseeable future.

Sadly, the news media aren't the only groups within America that have misplaced their priorities. To the detriment of this nation, there are many other groups, two in particular, that have not only misplaced their priorities, but had a major hand in this last election. I'm referring to neither the Republicans nor the Democrats. Those to whom I refer belong to either the Green or Blind Parties.

The first of these two major groups is apparently more concerned with the color green—green, as in something other than an individual from another planet or the purveyor of marijuana. However, after hearing of some of the antics of this group of people, one could logically opine that they are indeed from another world or have consumed their fair share of this illegal household plant.

The people in this group refer to themselves as environmentalists, while a good many others affectionately refer to them as "tree huggers." I, on the other hand, call these people the modern-day Nostradamuses. While running around playing Chicken Little, they have gotten many of us to believe that they and they alone are going to save us from ourselves. In their opinion, if we, not only as a nation but as a world, don't soon change our ways, the Earth as we now know it shall be reduced to nothing more than a big ball of fire. But when?

According to them, this could happen in about 100 years. Therefore, while these people are putting much, if not all, of their time and effort into something that may or may not happen a century away, the country they are attempting to save is rapidly being removed—not by erosion, but by those here illegally in search of a better life. Moreover, while they maintain their focus so far away, they are failing to realize that, should the economy stay upon its current path, they shall have no money to save the Earth.

In fairness to this group, after reading several reports and watching many television programs on such things as global warming, I think some of their predictions have merit. As none of their issues appears to be imminent, I, for one, shall place my focus upon less important issues such as our economy.

Until this group can convince me that their issues are of utmost importance, I shall continue to put as much credence in their claims as I do in the words emitting from the mouth of the mentally ill and inebriated man who stands upon the nearest street corner and, holding a Bible, informs us all that the world is about to end.

Speaking of the Bible, I now come to the second of these two major groups, the Blind Party. Members of this party prefer to be called the religious right; many others refer to them as Bible-thumpers. This group is in many ways similar to the Green Party, but has one major difference. Whereas the Green Party's priorities are set upon scientific evidence, the Blind Party's priorities are set forth by a man that no one in this party has ever seen or met. He is also a man whom members of this group themselves would heavily criticize because of the length of his hair and the way he dressed. They not only live their lives in accordance to the law as set forth by the Son of the Invisible Man, who himself is invisible but they are very critical of those who do not. This group is made up of many different faiths, so at times, they end up criticizing themselves.

In many of these so-called faiths, gambling is forbidden, which I myself find both humorous and hypocritical. To me, these people aren't only Bible-thumpers, they are the ultimate riverboat gamblers. Specifically, if these same people were to play in a full-ring game of Texas Hold'em, they would undoubtedly, without first looking at their hole cards, commit their entire bankroll (their lives in this case), to the middle.

Simply put, these individuals live in a way in which they forfeit much of their daily lives in hopes of a better life elsewhere—again, a place no one has ever seen. In my opinion, those who choose to live by these so-called laws are no different from or better than the individual who chooses to drive a fertilizer truck at a very high rate of speed toward a building. They too are betting everything on a better life elsewhere.

As I have previously said, this party is made up of various faiths, each having its own set of laws and/or ideals. Although I had no intention of singling out any one faith, I have to, not only because it is relevant to the subject of this book, but all of the owners of my company are members of this faith.

The company, rather faith, that I am referring to is the Church of Jesus Christ of Latter-day Saints, better known to many as the Mormons. This faith, in my opinion, is by far the least understood and, as a result, gets a bad rap. Just as with many other faiths, Mormons believe and act in ways that I agree with as well as in ways that I do not.

However, in view of the low number of current recruits, our military can take a recruiting lesson from the Mormon Church. The Mormons have done such a good job with their worldwide recruitment effort that it has essentially come full circle and has in a sense come back to, for lack of a better phrase, bite them on the ass.

Salt Lake City, Utah, if you aren't already aware, is where the headquarters of the Mormon Church is located. I haven't a clue as to how they came about settling in Salt Lake City, but if I had to venture a guess, Brigham Young became tired during his trek from the East Coast to the West and didn't want to travel any farther.

Nevertheless, Salt Lake City is no longer known solely as the headquarters of the Mormon Church. According to recent reports, it is rapidly becoming America's gangland. It seems that many of their young members are setting down their Bibles shortly after service on Sunday in favor of guns, knives, and/or chains.

Cities being overrun by gangs is neither new nor unique. The gang problem facing this city, however, is. To be more specific, this problem is "homegrown." Many of those who relocated to this "Holy Land" in order to join one of its many gangs are the offspring of those whom the Mormon Church had recruited from abroad. In the unlikely event that this city is indeed overrun by these gangs, the Mormon Church has only itself to blame.

Those who own my company are members in good standing of this faith. In fact, they pride themselves on being those who strictly comply with those laws as set forth by Joseph Smith (first CEO of the Mormon Church) and company. They are so compliant, I can honestly say that I have never witnessed any one of these individuals smoke, consume an adult beverage, or attend a movie with an R rating or above. Moreover, they think so much of the Mormon Church, they have modeled their own business after it.

One would only need to go down the roster of those this company employs to see that it has a recruiting program that mirrors the one of their church. There is, however, one big exception. Whereas the Mormon Church has done its best to give away a city, this company, without anyone's consent, is currently attempting to give away this country.

These owners are not only greedy, but arrogant as well. Their employment of illegal immigrants indicates that they believe that the laws of their church supersede the laws put forth by this nation. Although I cannot say for certain, I can only assume that the employment of illegal immigrants is not frowned upon by their church. Honestly, I would not be surprised in the least bit if the church itself encourages this practice.

Some may think that I may be off base with this allegation. Others may even be appalled by it. Either way, I assure you that this allegation is not as far-fetched as it may seem. In this case, the hiring of illegal immigrants benefits both my employer as well as the Mormon Church. Although those who own my company would have you believe that they have been forced to hire these individuals, in all reality, the reason they do is in order to pad their own bankroll. The more money my employer makes, the more money their church makes in the form of tithing. That money can then be used by the church to recruit more church—or gang—members.

That being said, I personally have nothing against those who practice this faith. In fact, they act in a way that if I had acted in that same way, my life might have turned out better than it has already. So in the coming years, I have decided to consume a little less caffeine, smoke fewer cigars, and dress a little more appropriately.

Unfortunately for this nation, those members of the Green Party will most likely continue to live in the future, and those who live their lives according to the teachings of their faiths may in the end find out that the book they strictly adhere to could very well contain more fiction than a Stephen King novel. Until the members of both of these parties begin to live in the moment, our nation will continue to be occupied by those who shouldn't be here.

In addition to these groups, individuals have even gotten into the act. There are individuals within this nation who have not only misplaced their priorities, but have even gone so far as to do everything within their power to ensure they get their fifteen minutes of fame. If there ever were such an award, the following individual would get my vote for the "Andy Warhol":

At some point, I had all the compassion in the world for this recipient, then she opened her mouth. In doing so, she has, in my opinion, thrown the proverbial baby out with the bath water. In fact, any compassion I had for her is now gone. For those of you who may be wondering, this recipient's name is Cindy Sheehan, who, like me, is a resident of the state of California. I do, however, have information that for a brief period of time, she relocated to Texas in close proximity to then President Bush. Presumably she did so in order to get across whatever point she was attempting to make.

Ms. Sheehan, it seems, has a good portion of this nation believing, as the Metallica song "One" starts off, that she gave her only begotten son in the defense of this nation. Moreover, Ms. Sheehan, along with her band of bleeding-heart liberals, has her followers believing that her son lost his life because of a vendetta that President Bush had with another country and its leader.

Whether or not this is true, and in the hopes of not sounding crass, I believe Ms. Sheehan did not give up her only begotten son. Unless I am mistaken and unless her son had a gun pointed at his head until he enlisted, it was he who voluntarily gave up his life. Being a former Marine myself, I am well aware of the great lengths the Marine Corps goes to to explain to those who want to enlist that by signing the enlistment contract, they are possibly signing their own death warrant.

Her actions are indicative of a person who is both selfish and unaware. I use the word "unaware" here instead of "ignorant" and/or "stupid" out of respect for my late mother, Barbara, the woman who had to constantly remind me that I need to treat others as I want to be treated. Since I have no desire whatsoever to be known as an ignorant or stupid person, I shall continue to refer to Ms. Sheehan as one who is greatly unaware.

Her acting the way she does shows that she has either forgotten or just doesn't know who has made it possible to do the things that she does. What I believe she has failed to realize is that she is neither the first nor sadly the last parent who has ever lost a son or daughter as the cost of freedom she along with millions of other Americans enjoy on a daily basis. After coming to the realization that she isn't the only parent who has lost a child, she then needs to either pick up a history book or go back to school in order to raise her awareness.

Maybe then she will be able to direct her anger toward those responsible for declaring the war that took the life of her son. In doing so, she will then discover what many of us already know, unless I am gravely mistaken or former President Bush had indeed found a way around the Constitution (as many Americans have accused his father, George H.W., of doing), that regardless of his proclivity for "wanting" to go to war with Iraq, I have been led to believe he could not have declared war without the approval of the Congress. If that is true and since Congress is composed of individuals elected by us, she needs to point her finger at the American public as a whole rather than wasting her and our time blaming Bush.

That being said, I want the reader to be cognizant of the fact that I am neither for nor against the war in Iraq. I am, however, of the belief that when the president of the United States says jump, we as Americans should jump, or as we used to say in the Marine Corps, it's not our job to question why, it's our job to do or die.

I have to assume that whoever was responsible for declaring war took no pleasure in doing so. Moreover, I have faith that my government had information that was not disseminated to the general public that this war was then and is still necessary. Furthermore, I need not remind the reader that history has shown that war, unlike the checks sent out by the Bush administration, stimulates our economy.

If by chance, Ms. Sheehan, you're reading this book, I am not only sorry for your loss, but am very appreciative of the fact your son had the intestinal fortitude to defend the freedoms I currently enjoy. Obtaining the limelight you desperately sought has come at the expense of dividing the nation your son lost his life defending. Moreover, while you were enjoying your fifteen minutes of fame, things such as jobs were being taken by illegal immigrants and these same immigrants where utilizing services they were not entitled to use.

This year, as I have done so forty-nine times before, I am going to celebrate my birth. Invisible Man willing, I shall celebrate many more. Realistically, statistics as well as my family history indicate that I have more life behind me than I do in front of me.

In my opinion, people of my generation and older are less likely to concern themselves with the views of the environmentalists. In fact, I assume people in my age bracket tend to concentrate on the matters at hand, such as the economy. Some may even, if they have not already, become a member of the Blind Party as their lives are nearing their conclusion.

The other day, while going over some notes from another book I am entertaining the thought of writing, I was reminded that the future of this nation is really not in my hands or the hands of my generation. During this review, I came across notes that I maintained on a general court-martial that was held aboard Camp Pendleton for a Marine who was to have allegedly molested his child.

Whether or not this individual was found guilty is irrelevant here. What is, however, is the very unorthodox closing argument that was delivered by the prosecuting attorney. It was during this closing argument that this attorney decided to switch professions by becoming a disc jockey. His new profession was, however, short-lived. It was so short that he had played only the first line from Whitney Houston's song, "Greatest Love of All."

For those who are unfamiliar with this song, the first line and I shall paraphrase here, goes "Children are our future, treat them well." These words are true and they reminded me of several conversations I have had in the recent past with one of these "children."

This young man goes by the name of James. He gets paid to pitch (deal, for those who are unfamiliar with gambling terminology) cards at a club in Oceanside, California. His outward appearance is immaculate, and he appears to be either well-read and/or educated. Surely he has made his parents proud, and if he was to be used as a measuring stick with regard to the future of this nation, we are indeed in good hands. So I thought.

Unfortunately, as I soon discovered, he, too, like many other Americans, has misplaced his priorities. This well-educated young man is of the belief that our failure to legalize marijuana is the most pressing problem facing this nation. In fact, he has no problem whatsoever telling those who are willing to listen his rationale as to why the use of marijuana should be legalized.

He is so well read on this subject that I have to admit that many of his arguments contain merit. He as well as other individuals such as comedian Bill Maher have even gone so far as to say that the legalization of this illegal houseplant would assist in bailing out our failing economy—an argument that clearly got my attention.

During this argument, he indicated that, based on the large number of individuals who currently use this substance, the government stands to make millions in revenue in the form of taxes from the sale of it. Moreover, it is also his belief that the legalization of marijuana is also a cost-saving measure. Specifically, by legalizing this drug, the government can save millions in salaries by hiring less DEA agents.

I agree in part. However, those who currently supplement their income by the sale of this substance have already shown a willingness to break the law. A valid argument could then be made that these same individuals would not, in order to make more profit, report all of their sales. Therefore, despite what those individuals in favor of this argument would have you believe, for every dollar made in the taxation of this drug, another will be lost by not reporting its sale.

Assuming every sale would be reported by these same individuals is in so many ways like performing a background check on the immigrant who is already here illegally. It's senseless. That illegal immigrant has also shown his or her willingness to break our laws. Therefore, a clean background check from his native country is, in my opinion, irrelevant.

As we all know, marijuana is a hallucinogen. So I guess those who believe that its legalization is of utmost importance to this nation are of the belief that the problems of this nation will be solved while they are under its influence. Moreover, many of these users may be in favor of illegal immigration, as along with these illegal immigrants comes the drug that feeds their habit.

There is one other point of interest that I would like to bring to the attention of my fellow users who are adamantly in favor of the legalization of this drug. Just as the government has been able to restrict the content in alcohol, I'm certain the government will find a way to restrict the amount of THC (the drug contained within marijuana) for our consumption if it is legalized.

The bottom line is that we need to treat the United States as if it were a patient—a patient that had just been wheeled into the emergency room after sustaining multiple injuries as the result a motor vehicle accident. Even to someone such as me, whose medical expertise is grossly limited to taking an aspirin for a headache or simply placing a Band-Aid upon a minor cut or scrape, it is obvious that in order to save the patient the attending physician must first determine which of those injuries must be treated first. Those treating the minor injuries first, I assume, run a greater risk of either causing more harm or death to the patient.

I admit that some of those issues as set forth above are indeed serious and, at some point, need and should be addressed. However, fixing these and those that I personally feel are unimportant without first fixing the problem of illegal immigration is like attempting to repair a flat tire by first filling it with air. It just isn't going to work!

CHAPTER IX

Change Is Inevitable

(Except From a Vending Machine)

After you've done a thing the same way for two years, look it over carefully. After five years, look at it with suspicion. And after ten years, throw it away and start all over.
Alfred Edward Perlman, prominent railroad president

DURING HIS INAUGURATION SPEECH OF 1933, PRESIDENT Franklin D. Roosevelt stood before the American public and said that the only thing we as a nation had to fear was fear itself. Words both profound and, as I have come to know, certainly words to live by. No matter how profound these words may be, however, they are, in a sense, easier said than done.

If life has taught me anything, it has taught me that fear is not what I and many other Americans fear most. If I had to venture a guess, it's change that we fear most. Death and marriage come to mind as the two biggest changes that one could and will possibly face during his or her lifetime. Death, in my opinion and it should go without saying, is the ultimate change.

Only those with essentially nothing to lose and those who know with certainty that a change will be for their betterment are fearless when it comes to change. Why is it, then, if fear is indeed the only thing that we as Americans should fear, we fear change the most? I have to assume that the reason we fear change is because it brings about, in more cases than not, the unknown.

It is my opinion that the majority of Americans have become complacent. Without change, these Americans find it easier to make decisions that will affect their daily lives. These individuals are of the belief that what had happened today will most likely again occur tomorrow.

However, as we have discovered, making the right change can indeed make our lives easier. Look at how far we have come, not only as a nation, but as a world, with the invention of such things as the cellular telephone and Internet. No longer are we confined to our homes awaiting that all-important telephone call. We also can, much to the displeasure of the local merchants, purchase things from halfway around the world with nothing more than a click of a button and a credit card.

In fact, had the cellular telephone been in existence when I was a child, I would have received less punishment—punishment (beatings, in my particular case) from a man who, had the child abuse laws that are currently in place today been in effect back then, would have gotten the death penalty.

Even the slightest of changes, many of which have gone unnoticed, have made our lives better. A prime example of this kind of change would be in the way we relieve ourselves. In the "old days," people relieved themselves outside of their homes, while they prepared and cooked their meals inside. Today, we relieve ourselves indoors, and it's not uncommon for many to cook their meals outdoors.

Our fear of change can be seen in both the minimal amount of times our Constitution has been amended and by those whom we elect into office. According to my count, and despite those who drafted it having had enough insight to realize that over time it would require change, the Constitution has been amended a mere 27 times. At the beginning, we gave ourselves such things as freedom of speech, protection from illegal search and seizure, as well as women the right to vote. Then, for whatever reason, in 1992, we stopped. Apparently, at that time, our elected officials were of the belief that we had indeed become the most perfect union or felt as if the world around us had stopped changing.

With regard to our elected officials, one only needs to go down a roster of those currently holding public office to discover that a few of these distinguished "gentlemen" seem to have been continuously re-elected into office since the first Continental Congress in 1775. Not only do these gentlemen represent the past but it wouldn't surprise me in the least bit if their personal physician employs the use of leeches in the treatment of disease.

Nevertheless, change for the most part requires an action rather than simply making a verbal statement. Many of us, however, are all talk and no action. In fact, when it comes to the subject of illegal immigration, a good majority of us do nothing more than complain as to the effect it has had upon this country and our economy. Yet when these same individuals are asked about proposing a change, presumably out of their fear of bringing on the unknown, they throw in the towel. Instead of proposing a change, they say things such as the floodgates have already been opened and it's too late to close them.

I believe it was Benjamin Franklin who first said that it is God who helps those who help themselves. We as citizens have ignored such advice and have pretty much left matters such as illegal immigration up to our elected officials. These elected officials, most likely out of their fear of change, or better yet fear that their wallets will be reduced, have also pretty much thrown in the towel with regard to illegal immigration.

While they were throwing in the towel, there were both organizations and individuals who have, to no avail, attempted to "help ourselves." One organization that comes to mind is the Social Security Administration. Recently I read in our local newspaper that the SSA had either attempted to or was getting ready to notify those employers who had sent in money that did not match up with the Social Security number it was sent under.

Although the article didn't specifically say, I have to assume their rationale for doing such was twofold. The first was to inform the employer that they may have committed an administrative error. The second reason may have been to put the employer on notice that they may indeed be employing an individual who isn't entitled to work here. Personally, I see nothing wrong with this course of action. In fact, as an American wage earner, I take comfort in knowing that my government, which takes money from me on a monthly basis, is also ensuring that it will be there for my use upon my retirement.

Not everyone, one individual in particular, shares this opinion. It seems as if a judge with the authority to do so stopped the Social Security Administration from sending out these notifications. Apparently, he felt that doing so violated the rights of those whose money did not match up with the number it was submitted under. Moreover, while I cannot remember the judge's name, I do remember that he had a Spanish surname.

This Hispanic judge is not, however, the only person who has prevented us from helping ourselves. In January 2008, in view of the fact that some cities within the state of California were adopting local laws that made it unlawful for landlords to rent to those here illegally, Governor Arnold Schwarzenegger signed into law a bill that prohibited landlords from asking for proof of citizenship or approval to be here. Interestingly enough, I was, up until that day, a huge supporter of the governor of the great state of California.

Many of you know, but if you don't, Governor Schwarzenegger is a naturalized citizen. Despite this fact, I voted for him in the last two elections. He had done such a great job, so I thought, that he even had me thinking that the United States Constitution needed to be amended in order that he, too, could run for the office of the president of the United States.

Based upon his actions of late, I now know why the framers of the world's strongest piece of paper (Constitution) made it a requirement that the president of the United States needed to be a natural-born citizen. Unfortunately, he has indeed shown his true colors, and with a little bit of luck, the only time the residents of the state of California will ever again hear the words "I'll be back" will be in a rerun of one of his movies.

In light of the foregoing, it is my belief that immediate changes are needed in order for us to "form and maintain a more perfect union"—changes that not only will undoubtedly bring the unknown, but are a crapshoot at best that they are for the betterment of this country.

Accordingly, here are the changes I believe are needed in order to make us a much better nation:

First and foremost, until each and every American who is not only able but also willing to work is employed, all applications for entrance into this country should be denied. The medical profession seems to be being overrun by those from other countries. While I can't speak for others, doctors who are born here and speak fluent English are hard enough to understand as it is.

There is, in my opinion, more than sufficient evidence to indicate that the Electoral College currently in place has long since outlived both its purpose and effectiveness. Its outdatedness has not only taken away our voice but has discouraged many of us from voting. A prime example of this was the 2008 election. Although I had no intention of casting my vote for any of those running for the office of president, the national news media had reported that a candidate had already "won" my state prior to my leaving my residence and heading to the voting booth. So, in order to not only get our voice back but to get us back out to vote, which will allow us to help ourselves get rid of problems such as illegal immigration, we need to do away with the Electoral College in its entirety.

Next, someone who is very near and dear to my heart once gave me the advice that I should always "say what I mean and mean what I say." Utilizing that wisdom, we should then require those Americans who feel a need to say "until death do us part" to mean it.

Specifically, anyone who marries an immigrant should be required to, with the exception of physical abuse and/or rape, stay married until death does, in fact, part them. Hopefully, this change alone will discourage those currently entertaining the thought of marrying for the sole purpose of obtaining a green card for another from doing so.

A law with wording similar to the one that prohibits those Americans who at some point of their lives were convicted of a felony from voting and/or possessing a firearm needs to be put into effect. Specifically, those Americans who, with or without their knowledge, have either personally employed, owned or had an interest in a company that employs or has employed, or whose political candidacy is now or has previously been financed by an illegal immigrant should be permanently prohibited from running for or holding any public office.

Most importantly, the Constitution with regard to citizenship needs to be amended. We need to treat those children born from parents who are illegally here the same way we do the evidence that has been obtained from an illegal search. Since both are the fruit from a poisonous tree, neither should be admissible. Specifically it should be amended to exclude citizenship for those children who are born upon our soil from illegal immigrants.

Now that I have identified the root of the problem of our failing nation and recommended courses of action to correct it, we can proceed with ridding ourselves of the problem of illegal immigration. The following chapter will set forth my recommendations for doing such.

CHAPTER X

If You're Not Part of the Solution, You're Part of the Problem

(The Melting Pot Hath Runneth Over)

What we're saying today is that you're either part
of the solution or you're part of the problem.
Eldridge Cleaver, author

We can't solve problems by using the same kind of thinking
we used when we created them.
Albert Einstein, theoretical physicist

Desperate diseases must have desperate remedies.
Proverb

EMPLOYERS, LIKE EVERYONE ELSE IN AMERICA THESE DAYS, RE-fuse to take responsibility for their own actions. In my opinion, we have sat upon our laurels far too long and it seems as if the greatest nation in the world has gotten up and quit. It also appears that we as a nation would rather whine about threatening issues rather than taking any action whatsoever. In doing so, we are not only losing control of this nation that many have lost their lives defending, but we are actually promoting those issues we intend to eradicate.

Not everyone, however, has sat back and let this nation go to those here illegally. For instance, sometime during 2007, a bill we now refer to as the Secure Borders, Economic Opportunity and Immigration Reform Act was put before Congress for approval. Had I been consulted prior to its submission, I would have renamed it the "If you can't beat them, join them" bill. Nevertheless, it is my understanding that those who drafted this act called for the amnesty of those immigrants who are here illegally and are able to prove they have been continuously employed within the United States of America for the last ten years. The act further went on to state that after receiving amnesty for their misconduct, these same individuals, if they so chose, could then apply for American citizenship by simply filling out forms and paying the appropriate fees.

This bill and/or act, in my opinion, would have solved nothing. If it did anything, it would have taken those who unlawfully hire illegal immigrants off the hook for their misconduct and, despite what the framers of this bill would have had you believe, it would have given hope to those not yet here who are entertaining the thought of unlawfully entering this country in order to obtain employment and citizenship.

I, however, must demur. While I agree that this bill did address the issue of those already illegally employed, its wording was no different from the bill regarding illegal immigration that was passed in 1986 that also gave millions of illegal immigrants amnesty. Moreover, it was a copycat of the amnesty bill signed by President Carter for those "draft dodgers" who didn't have the backbone to defend the freedoms that many of them enjoy today.

Even my employer, who hires illegal immigrants, has a solution to this problem. Unlike the bill that was before Congress in 2007, his suggestion does not include the possibility of citizenship for those he and others like him unlawfully employ. He suggests that, rather than offering these individuals the opportunity of becoming a citizen, they be given nothing more than amnesty and a work visa. That way, the illegal immigrant can continue to work without the benefits of being a United States citizen.

Hopefully, you're laughing as hard as I did when I first heard him utter these words. This man is far from stupid, so surely he must be aware that such a suggestion would benefit only those such as himself who employ illegal immigrants. If something as ridiculous as this is passed, employers will still be allowed to pay these individuals poorly with little or no benefits. In other words, he himself is asking for amnesty from prosecution for unlawfully hiring illegal immigrants.

Speaking of ridiculous, a friend of mine who gets paid to repair our presses had a solution that at first I thought was absurd. However, after careful consideration, I found that, while absurd, if implemented, it might not entirely stop illegal immigration, but it does, however, have the possibility of slowing it down.

He suggested that the states bordering the country of Mexico should be directed to dig a trench at least one mile wide and one hundred feet deep. Subsequently, the trench should be filled with water and that the earth removed in making the ditch then be transported to the City of New Orleans. In exchange for this earth, the City of New Orleans would send alligators to those border states for placement in the ditch.

Granted, this solution does not address those people already here illegally; it does, however, address the issue of future illegal immigration. If this solution is one thing, it's humorous to say the least. It doesn't stand a chance of being passed, not because it's absurd, but because of the money and manpower needed to implement it. Using the logic of my late mother, Barbara, this solution is not as absurd as it appears. Specifically, my mother used to tell me, "If you don't like something, change it; if you can't change it, change the way you feel about it."

In light of this statement, we Americans need not think of the money being spent; rather, we should be looking at the money being saved by stopping those coming illegally from the south to take our jobs and use our services. In my opinion, that would be money well spent. More importantly for the people of New Orleans, they then can take the earth they received in exchange for their alligators and reinforce their current levees and build new ones to protect them from future disasters as well.

As you can see, I am not the only one with a solution to the illegal immigration problem that this nation currently faces. But that's not what this book is about. It's about my solutions, and I have but two, one of which you may or may not consider as absurd as my friend's. Regardless of your opinion, both solutions will not only address those already here, but will drastically, if not entirely, stop illegal immigration in the future.

Before I state my first solution, I must caution the readers that if they choose to take matters into their own hands after reading this first solution, chances are they stand a better than fair chance of ending up in prison or could possibly receive the death penalty. That being said, my first solution is as follows:

Shoot them. That's right, I said shoot them. My reading and subsequent understanding of the Second Amendment to the U.S. Constitution gives me the right to bear arms. In other words, I have the right to own a firearm. That being said, the only question that remains is why anyone would possess a firearm. I can think of only three, which I shall list in reverse order of what I feel to be their importance.

The last reason as to why anyone would own a firearm is to commit a crime. I'm pretty sure, but not certain, that the framers of this amendment did not have committing a crime in mind when they drafted this amendment, nor am I suggesting that one go out and commit one. Some, after reading this, may opine that I'm doing just that.

Another reason to own a firearm is for recreational purposes. This is where gun "nuts" such as the late Charlton Heston, along with all the other card-carrying NRA members, have found a loophole. While the thought of killing a defenseless animal or putting a bullet hole in a piece of paper does nothing for me, it apparently does give others some amount of enjoyment. In their defense, they could argue that by doing such, they are sharpening their marksmanship skills in the event they are called to active duty to defend our country, an argument clearly within the framework of the Second Amendment. Although the thought has crossed my mind, I am not proposing that the shooting of illegal immigrants be classified as a sport; it would, however, make for an interesting video game.

Now I come to what I believe the framers considered the only reason to own a firearm. Self-defense—in layman's terms, protecting what is rightfully ours. It is here where I find justification for not only shooting but killing anyone illegally in this country. It is for self-preservation that I believe the Second Amendment was put into place. Specifically, this amendment was written in order to provide weapons to those left behind as a second line of defense during a time of war. Moreover, this amendment made it possible for these same individuals to provide food for their families while honing their marksmanship skills.

In support of the above, the Second Amendment, since its inception, has been cited by many attorneys in their defense of a client who had been on trial for the shooting and/or killing of an individual who had entered his or her home unlawfully. Moreover, because of the Second Amendment, some states have even adopted laws that prohibit the prosecution of those who do shoot and/or kill such an individual under certain circumstances. Some of these circumstances include being in fear of one's life or the life of one of his family members and/or the prevention of damage or loss of his or her personal property.

As absurd as it might sound, it is my belief that the same protection should apply to those individuals who shoot and possibly kill those who are currently in this country illegally. The fact remains that, whether or not one is a homeowner, he or she is entitled to claim the United States as his or her home. Moreover, it is my contention that when someone enters this country illegally for the purpose of obtaining employment and/or receiving services such as WIC, they are no different from someone breaking into someone's residence.

This solution, unlike those stated above, not only addresses those who are currently here illegally, but it also sends a very strong message to those entertaining the idea of coming here illegally. It would also be good for the economy. Gun and gun supplies sales will increase, and unemployed Americans will be able to secure employment that is currently filled by illegal immigrants, which we all know would reduce the current unemployment rate.

Also, it does not require a great deal of taxpayers' money to implement. In fact, it has the potential of saving money. Specifically, there would be no need to hire border patrolmen; instead, it would cost only a few hundred dollars to post signs that read "Trespassers will be shot, enter at your own risk," an expense I'm willing to pay out of my own pocket if approved.

It does, however, contain a fatal flaw. There is no ironclad way of determining who is here legally from those who are not just by looking at them. Unfortunately, if something like this was implemented, the possibility of killing an innocent person would be far too great.

Now I come to the last of my two solutions: a solution that I believe will bring illegal immigration to a complete halt, a solution that will not only NOT cost the American taxpayer money, but will be opposed only by those who are currently making millions off of the illegal immigration issue.

The solution is so simple that I'm surprised no one has suggested it. To rid ourselves of the problem of illegal immigration, we need only to make those responsible for creating it accountable.

If this solution ever made it to Congress and it needed a name, I would call it the "You made the mess, you clean it up" bill. It is those individuals or organizations that hire illegal immigrants that I believe to be the problem rather than the solution. My solution requires these same individuals or organizations to clean up their own mess. This solution will not only address those already here illegally but will prevent others from coming over here with the intent of coming away with a piece of the American dream. It can also be put into place without enacting any new laws or using any taxpayers' money that should be utilized elsewhere. Moreover, if approved, it will not only lower health and auto insurance but will greatly help out the failing Social Security Administration. Now comes the trillion-dollar question of how.

First and foremost, those who hire illegal immigrants must be made responsible for any and all actions taken by the illegal immigrant. We should hold the individual or organization as if they brought them to this country for their own purpose whether they did or not. For example, the state of California requires anyone who operates a motor vehicle to have a license and insurance. This protects the driver and others who may be harmed due to the driver's negligence.

Insurance companies, presumably after paying out millions of dollars for damages not incurred by their insured, changed their underwriting standards. In the past, those cases in which their insured caused the damage, the insurance carriers recouped (although they deny such an allegation) from their insured by raising either their deductible or monthly premiums, and in some cases both. For those cases in which their insured was not at fault, the insurance carrier filed claim against the negligent party's insurance carrier. So, what happened when the party at fault had no insurance, as is the case with all illegal immigrants?

The insurance carrier whose driver was not at fault ended up picking up the entire tab without any recourse to recoup this money. But those were the good old days. The insurance carriers caught on to this and created what the state of California now calls uninsured motorist insurance. Basically, this coverage protects the insured from paying out of pocket for damages that they may incur at no fault of their own and from someone not insured. In other words, if the insured for whatever reason, elected not to pay for this coverage and he or she then incurs damage from a vehicle not insured, his insurance carrier is under no obligation to assist them. These "innocent" people are oftentimes left without the use of their vehicle because they cannot afford to pay for the repairs. The loss of this vehicle, in many cases, hinders them from getting to and from work.

I'm in no way suggesting that all uninsured motorists are illegal immigrants; however, if only one is, it's one too many. I am suggesting, however, that, if that one individual who is here illegally is involved in an accident without insurance, and he or she is unable to pay for the damage, the person or organization who employs the individual should be held accountable for the damage. The increasing cost of auto insurance is not entirely the fault of those who unlawfully employ illegal immigrants, but they have increased the chance of our being hit by an uninsured motorist. Insurance carriers have realized this and have raised their premiums accordingly. Requiring those who employ illegal immigrants to pay for damages incurred by them will not only rid ourselves of the problem of illegal immigration but will greatly reduce the amount of money we pay, thus saving Americans millions of dollars per year.

This same principle should be applied when it comes to medical services and those agencies that are funded by the American tax dollar. If an illegal immigrant is in need of medical services and is unable to pay, then, again, the individual or organization that employs them should be required to pay. If an illegal immigrant utilizes the WIC program, for example, the employer should be made to reimburse the program. In doing so, there will be more for those who rightly deserve these services. Moreover, it will also save the American taxpayer millions of dollars per year.

The American people have not only lost jobs, benefits, and paid more in insurance, but, in some cases, have lost their lives at the hands of illegal immigrants. In 2003, Tony Zeppetella, a young law enforcement officer, was gunned down in Oceanside, California, by such an individual. The question is, why did this peace officer lose his life? He lost his life because some greedy employer chose to pad his profits by hiring this guy.

In cases such as this, I believe an eye for an eye is in order. If we were to make the person who hires illegal immigrants responsible for the crimes they commit, and in the case of this officer's murder, sentence him to death, or better yet a member of his family, I wonder if that employer would have hired this individual and, if he had not, that law enforcement officer would still be here today. I just don't know. I do know, however, if he wouldn't still be here, it wouldn't be because of that illegal immigrant.

If we do nothing more, making the employer responsible for every action of those they employ illegally will, in my opinion, greatly slow down illegal immigration. But we simply cannot stop here, nor can we forget that those who hire illegal immigrants are breaking the law, and if caught and subsequently convicted, should be punished. This can be accomplished by what I believe to be the most powerful law currently on the books.

It has been used to take down major drug dealers, motorcycle clubs, as well as high-ranking organized crime members. The law that I'm referring to is the RICO Act, more commonly known as the organized crime bill. Although I'm no expert when it comes to this act, I do know that in order for one to be convicted, the person or organization must be organized, in other words, have some sort of chain of command. Unless I'm mistaken, most companies have a chain of command, e.g., president, vice president, chief executive officer, etc. Therefore, most companies fall within the framework of this act.

This act not only has the authority to convict and punish, but it also has the authority to seize any and all money and property obtained from an illegal act. Additionally, I'm led to believe that the property seized as the result of this act is then auctioned off and the money from those auctions is distributed among various government agencies. Those who employ illegal immigrants, with or without knowledge, should be prosecuted pursuant to this act, and, if convicted, serving time and paying substantial fines is simply not enough.

Property such as land, buildings, machinery, and all profits should be seized and subsequently auctioned off. The proceeds from the auction as well as all profits seized should then be given to the failing Social Security Administration in hopes of providing for those hardworking Americans who may not have anything to show for their hard work.

One last point I'd like to make before wrapping up this chapter is that the opposition to this solution—those who employ illegal immigrants—will be the first ones to cry foul.

They will argue it simply isn't fair to them. They will insist there is no ironclad way of verifying someone's immigration status. Further, they will tell us that it will cost the American taxpayer millions in order to start a registry to verify those who are seeking employment.

That's nonsense! These people are asking for something that ought to be coming out of their own pockets. Moreover, they will also tell you it isn't fair they risk losing everything they own because someone lied in order to obtain employment. In my opinion, that is nothing more than the price of doing business. In addition, I've been told that ignorance of the law is no excuse, and that should be the case when it comes to the hiring of illegal immigrants. It only stands to reason that if someone stood a chance of losing everything he owned, he would take every precaution to ensure he didn't.

It is common practice that most employers, either by phone or in writing, verify prospective employee references. The same effort should be applied when verifying someone's immigration status. How hard and expensive could it be? A birth certificate is a public record and can be viewed or purchased by anyone for a minimum fee, which in most cases is no more than $15.

In those cases where the prospective employee was born outside of the United States, he or she should either have in his possession a resident green card, a resident alien card, or a work visa. All three documents, I believe, are issued by the same government agency and in most cases can be verified with one phone call. For those cases in which the prospective employee cannot produce any of the aforementioned documentation, there stands a good chance he or she is not here legally and should not be hired under any circumstances. However, should the employer hire the individual on the chance he or she might be here legally, then, in my opinion, he does so willfully and stands the chance of losing everything.

There is only one thing standing in the way of this solution or something similar—getting Congress' approval. It is my belief that there aren't enough elected officials who do not own a business that employs illegal immigrants, have an interest in such, or better yet whose campaign isn't financed by one.

In summary, while acknowledging nothing is ever foolproof, I'm willing to bet there isn't one employer alive willing to risk everything he owns or the life of a loved one over the hiring of an illegal immigrant. In the event that such an individual does exist, I am certain that that person has to have his or her pants tailored to fit a set of brass balls that large.

Let's face it, people need money to survive, and in order to make money they need a job. If no one is willing to offer them a job or keep those currently employed, then, in my opinion, it only stands to reason that people will be less likely to come over here illegally, and if they do despite this, then by all means shoot them.

CHAPTER XI

No Man Is an Island

(I Get By With a Little Help From My Friends)

If your actions inspire others to dream more, learn more and become more, you are a leader.
John Quincy Adams, U.S. president

IN THE VERY FIRST CHAPTER OF THIS BOOK, I QUOTED MYSELF as saying "*I am who I am because of the decisions I have either made or not made throughout my life.*" While that statement is certainly true, it's not entirely true. I'm here today because of the help that I have received along the way from others, hence the title of this chapter.

I am, however, somewhat reluctant to list the names of those individuals who have provided me with such help, not because I don't think those people are deserving; rather, it is out of fear that I may erroneously omit someone. Despite this fear, I am reminded of a quote by our 27th president, William Taft, who once said, "*Failure to accord credit to anyone for what he may have done is a great weakness in any man.*"

More importantly, failing to acknowledge those who have helped, I would, in a sense, be doing something I have been very critical of both the United States and my local government of doing. Specifically, it would show that I am more concerned with the feelings of the few rather than the whole.

Nevertheless, in the words of President John Qunicy Adams that I have set forth on the preceding page, the following individuals are my leaders:

Charles W. Padget - The only man I have ever known who truly possessed the wisdom of Solomon. What I am about to say now is something I wish I had been man enough to say while he was alive: *"I Love You, Dad."*

Barbara E. Padget - The strongest woman I have ever met. Then again, with both my father and me in the house, she had to be. Unlike many others in my life, she didn't die, she simply relocated and became a permanent resident of my heart.

Barbara Kinner - My "adopted" mom. Although I truly wish we had met under better circumstances, I shall forever be grateful for your friendship. You have always been there for me, when I should have been there for you. In fact, I doubt that I would have gotten through these past three years without your guidance and support. Moreover, there isn't a snowball's chance in hell of my ever repaying you for everything you have done for me. So, rather than try, I'm going to ask you to do one more thing for me: Find that man in your life you so richly deserve, one who not only complements your life but brings you the joy and happiness so much like that which your daughter brought me.

Susan Bagnasco-Fox - For the past couple of months, I have gone back and forth trying to decide whether or not I should even write this. In doing so, I realized that when it is all said and done, I would regret it if I didn't. So here it is. You are the reason I was able to finish this book. You are the reason for who I am now and who I shall become in the future. In fact, you are all my reasons. Unfortunately, you mucked your hand prior to either of us seeing the "river." Because, as certain as the sun will come up tomorrow, had I had the chance of seeing that card—revealing our future—I would have committed my entire bankroll to the middle before the river card had the chance of hitting the felt. For what it's worth, you are now and shall forever be the one I can't live without.

Tiffany M. Kinner - Had death not torn the pages all away, this would have been one of the greatest stories ever told. Since that fateful night, a single day has not passed in which I have not only wondered what might have been but who you'd be today. As the song goes, some days I not only miss your smile, but on those days when the sky is indeed blue, I feel that I can in fact talk to you. Nevertheless, my sun shall continue to rise and set with the memory of you.

Bryan & Gisela Aguilar - If wealth were measured by friendship, then because of you both, I am indeed the world's wealthiest man. You took a chance on me when no one else was willing. I hope someday that I shall be able to repay you both in kind.

Shannon Hatton - The dilemma here is what could I possibly say to you that no other man has. "Keep your clothes on" is unfortunately about the only thing that comes to mind. All kidding aside, you, in a way only you could do, made crazy seem sane for me. Your sick and twisted humor kept me forging on. At times, when I was going to give up, you somehow made me find hope in my hopelessness.

Jennifer (last name withheld upon her request) - Had I known that women of your caliber existed in New York, I would have never left. Your compassion and encouragement have gotten me through a lot of tough times. It did not, however, go unnoticed and I shall forever cherish our friendship.

Mister (Rick) Smith - My sounding board. I know I was preaching to the choir on this one, but thanks nonetheless.

Jackie Logue - Wordsmith by trade, my Hemingway. Without you, this book would be nothing more than a bunch of misplaced, misspelled words.

Andrew Todd and Nicholas Charles Padget - Sadly or shall I say, pathetically, there was a point in my life when I chose a bottle of Budweiser over my children. My weakness has come at your expense. I wish not only that someday you will both come to forgive me but sincerely hope you have become something I wasn't—a man.

Ron Walker - I have in the past made a living at reading people at the card table. My initial read that you could be counted upon for your candor was correct. Your opinion was both valued and greatly appreciated. At the minimum, you are indeed a breath of fresh air.

Howard "Rusty" Coones and W. Eric Repik - While many others would have given up, the actions and courage of you both have proved that it is not only possible for one to pay his or her debt to society, but it's also possible to make something of himself afterward. You are indeed an inspiration to each and every one of us who are currently on the downside of advantage.

Rebecca Pantuso - Although it was only for a brief moment, you were my Juliet, and hopefully, I, your Romeo. Individuals from different sides of the tracks, indeed. Recently, I have come to realize you were right. A man needs love; and love is denied expression by poverty. A poor man who has nothing to give cannot fill his place as a husband, father, or as a man. Even though I didn't think it was possible, your intelligence far exceeds your beauty.

Deborah Holland - I too, have recently heard those dreaded words—"I love you, but I'm not in love with you." Not only were you not deserving of hearing them emit from my mouth, but you certainly deserved someone better than me. You possess everything a man could ever want in a woman. I guess one really doesn't know what he or she has until it's gone.

While there have been plenty of nights in my life that I will never remember, the following friends and family members I shall never forget:

Albert Padget; Margaret Padget; Richard Padget; Bonnie Paeth; Sandy Padget; Lisa Padget Brown; Christina Giglio; Erin Padget; Margie Stout; Merisue Repik; Wendy Blom; Hans Blom; Ed Repik; Gloria Repik; Nick Repik; Adam Repik; KO Coones; Rodrigo "T-Rod" Requejo; Neil Thompson; Bob Hutchinson; AJ Hutchinson; Dan Gallagher; Kathy Gallagher; Chris Tillman; Cindy Hazlett; Eddie Acobia; Janae Acobia; JoAnne Coolman; Maggie Jones; Jeffrey Burhop; Michael Biggs; Ron Zamir; Patricia O'Neal; Shirley Thieme Padget; Kathy Lake; Don Podgers; Colonel Mark L. Haiman, USMC Ret.; Captain Dale A. Dye, USMC Ret.; Philip G. Ulrich; Ed Sierra; Don Morton; Patrick Aguilar; Ben Aguilar; Jacob Glen; Scott Paeth; Peggy Campbell; Tom Paeth; Gil Harris; Mary Harris; Fred Barres; Carol Barres; Caroline Barres; Fred Barres; Jill "Chick" Harris; Lori Harris; Michelle Malone; Butch Porter; Jay Levine; Kaitlyn Tiponi Summer Aguilar; Denali Dunlap; Jeffrey Law; Moreland Choppers; everyone at Orange County Harley Davidson; Heather White; Colden Pipek; Nicole Barron; everyone at Ocean's Eleven Casino; and Bubba and Lilly.

Last, but not least, many, if not all of those reading this book may have noticed that nowhere within the preceding pages have I mentioned the name of the company in which I was employed for almost fifteen years.

Although I finally left this company to seek employment elsewhere since I began writing this book, if the truth be told, there is nothing more I would want to do than to stick it to those who have, in a sense, stuck it to me over the last fourteen-plus years. But since I have never dropped a dime on anyone in my life (tattled on someone, for those of you who are law-abiding citizens), I see no reason to make an exception here.

That being said, should anyone reading this book be in need of someone with almost fifteen years of printing experience, you have my consent to contact Royal Business Cards, located in Oceanside, California, in order to verify my employment history.

ABOUT THE AUTHOR

Charles Frederick Padget
(April 4, 1959 -   )

Born and rasied in Rochester, New York. A veteran of almost twelve years, he presently resides in Oceanside, California.

Mr. Padget currently divides his time between playing poker, books in progress, and riding Harleys.

THE NINES *Publishing*

Some publish *"How To"* books, others *"How To Think"* books, we publish only those that unequivocally *"Provoke Thought."*

Look for these other forthcoming thought provoking books from this soon-to-be best selling author.

LIVING WITH HEATHER

Mr. Padget describes in detail the time he had lived with Heather, a pretty, young and kept woman. In doing so, he not only discovered that some Americans are of the belief they are entitled to something for nothing, but are indeed paid by our government for doing it.

WHY COMMIT SUICIDE, WHEN YOU CAN BE HANGED FOR MURDER!

A novel that not only brings to light the flaws in the American justice system, but calls upon the carpet America's most notorious criminal—"The American Litigator."

The opinions expressed in this book or any thereafter are the views of the individual author and do not necessarily reflect the views and opinions of To The Nines Publishing. Those wishing to contact us may do so at *csr@2the9spub.com*. Those wanting to contact a particular author may either do so at the author's own personal contact information or by simply emailing them at *authors@2the9spub.com*.